KNIT HATS

with Woolly Wormhead

Published by Stackpole Books
An imprint of Globe Pequot the trade division of
The Rowman & Littlefield Pu_ hing Group, Inc.
4501 Forbes Blvd., Ste. 200
Lanham, MD 20706
www.stackpolebooks.com

Distributed by NATIONAL E OK NETWORK
800-462-6420

The original German edition was published as *Mützen Stricken*.
Copyright © 2019 frechverlag GmbH, Stuttgart, Germany (www.top-kreativ.de)
This edition is published by arrangement with Claudia Böhme Rights & Literary
Agency, Hannover, Germany (www.agency-boehme.com)

Photos: frechverlag GmbH, 70499 Stuttgart; Woolly Wormhead
Product Management: Mareike Upheber
Translation: Regina Sidabras, Berlin
Layout: Petra Theilfarth

We have made every effort to ensure the accuracy and completeness of these
instructions. We cannot, however, be responsible for human error, typographical
mistakes, or variations in individual work.

British Library Cataloguing in Publication Information available

Library of Congress Cataloging-in-Publication Data

Names: Woolly Wormhead, author.
Title: Knit hats with Woolly Wormhead / translation: Regina Sidabras,
    Berlin.
Other titles: Mützen Stricken. English
Description: Lanham, MD : Stackpole Books, an imprint of Rowman &
    Littlefield Publishing Group, Inc., (2021) | Translation of: Mützen
    Stricken. | Includes bibliographical references. | Summary:
    "International hat-knitting icon Woolly Wormhead is known for her
    unique, innovative hat designs. This collection of her work includes
    patterns for 22 of her designs"— Provided by publisher.
Identifiers: LCCN 2021004408 (print) | LCCN 2021004409 (ebook) | ISBN
    9780811739672 (paper ; permanent paper) | ISBN 9780811769594
    (electronic)
Subjects: LCSH: Knitting—Patterns. | Hats.
Classification: LCC TT825 .W6813 2021 (print) | LCC TT825 (ebook) | DDC
    746.43/2041—dc23
LC record available at https://lccn.loc.gov/2021004408
LC ebook record available at https://lccn.loc.gov/2021004409

♾™ The paper used in this publication meets the minimum requirements of
American National Standard for Information Sciences—Permanence of Paper for
Printed Library Materials, ANSI/NISO Z39.48-1992.

First Edition

KNIT HATS

with Woolly Wormhead

STYLES FOR THE WHOLE FAMILY

Stackpole
Books
Guilford, Connecticut

FOREWORD

WELCOME TO WOOLLY WORMHEAD'S WORLD OF HATS!

In this book, a compilation of unparalleled ideas by world-renowned designer Woolly Wormhead is waiting to be discovered by you. For her infallible intuition for unusual shapes and enthusiasm for innovations, Woolly was decorated with the British Crafts Award in 2018. Her designs are a tribute to her love of three-dimensional forms, which she has thoroughly explored and turned into easy-to-follow hand-knitting instructions.

Woolly's refined designs are cherished and revered by knitters, and they are appreciated by hat aficionados and proficient crafters as well. Her patterns, featuring intriguing construction solutions and unexpected turns, have more than a few surprises in store for you, so even accomplished hat knitters will never feel bored.

Woolly's aspiration to find the ideal hat for every head is reflected in the diversity of her designs. Since it takes a few tricks to create a perfectly fitting hat, this book includes a special chapter in which she shares her knowledge and expertise about selecting the correct shape and size.

To keep instructions as short as possible for this book, some abbreviations have been used. Abbreviations are divided into general terms that are used throughout the book and explained on page 119 and special ones that occur in only a few patterns and are explained within the instructions for the appropriate pattern.

Now, there is nothing like heading straight into the book and having fun exploring the unique designs! On the following pages, discover stunning new hat looks for her, him, and the kids. Time to get the needles clacking and to board the hat production train!

FOR HER

FOR HIM

FOR KIDS

THE BASICS

FOR HER

INFILARE

SIZES

To fit size: 18 (20, 22, 24) in./45.75 (51, 56, 61) cm

Finished size: 15.75 (17.5, 19.5, 21.25) in./40 (44.5, 49.5, 54) cm

YARN

226 (294, 370, 413) yd./207 (268, 338, 378) m sock weight (super fine), plied yarn

Additional 47 yd./43 m for a 6 × 6 in./15 × 15 cm swatch in St st

NEEDLES & NOTIONS

Set of US 2 (2.75 mm) DPNs or circular (or size needed to obtain gauge)

Spare needle or DPN for picking up sts

US C-2 (2.75 mm) crochet hook

Approx. 3 yd./3 m waste yarn

Stitch marker as necessary

Tapestry needle

SAMPLE DETAILS

Shown in Whimzy Sokkusu O (416 yd./380 m per 4.05 oz./115 g; 100% superwash merino)

Shown in size 22 in./56 cm on model with 21.25 in./54 cm circumference head

GAUGE

26 sts × 35 rows to 4 in./10 cm on US 2 (2.75 mm) needles over St st

26 sts × 80 rows to 4 in./10 cm on US 2 (2.75 mm) needles over tucked pattern

SKILLS REQUIRED

- knit and purl stitches
- knitting in the round
- increases and decreases
- provisional cast-on (see page 124)
- picking up stitches
- joining live stitches (see page 125)

HINTS

The tucks on the brim are designed to be tight and, as such, are fiddly to work. You may find it easier to pick up around 10 or 15 stitches at a time with either a short DPN or a cable needle ready for joining or to join one stitch at a time.

I also suggest you pick up the stitches from the first row of bumps (i.e., the reverse of the first round of stockinette stitch in each tuck), as this will make it easier to maintain the correct position. Alternatively, you could pick up the stitches from the reverse of last join round, which will make the brim even firmer and more decorative, but this approach will make the joining round tighter, too.

INSTRUCTIONS

Using waste yarn and provisional cast-on method, cast on 102 (114, 126, 138) sts. Change to main yarn and join in the round, being careful not to twist stitches. Place stitch marker to indicate start of round.

BRIM

Work stockinette stitch (knit every stitch) for five rounds. Next, slowly remove the provisional cast-on, stitch by stitch, and transfer all live stitches to spare needle—circular needles are best for this job. Holding both sets of needles and live stitches parallel, with WS together and RS facing you, you will join the brim tuck. Work the next round as follows:

Join rnd: *Knit next st from back needle together with the next st from the front needle; rep from * to end. 102 (114, 126, 138) sts

The first tuck has now been created. Now work a further five rounds of stockinette stitch.

MAKE TUCK

Using spare circular needle, pick up (but do not knit) 102 (114, 126, 138) sts from back of first knit round worked after the joining round (i.e., from the first round of single purl bumps on the WS of the work).

Holding both sets of needles parallel, with live stitches on the front needle and picked-up stitches on the back, with WS together and RS facing you, work the next round as follows:

Join rnd: *Knit stitch from back needle together with the stitch from the front needle; rep from * to end. 102 (114, 126, 138) sts

Work a further five rounds of stockinette stitch and repeat the tuck-making process (three tucks have been created so far).

Work a further five rounds of stockinette stitch and repeat the tuck-making process by picking up the stitches from the purl bumps on the reverse of the first of the five rounds. This last tuck will be joined differently; work join round as follows to also incorporate increases for the body:

Brim join/inc rnd: *K1 from back needle, k1 from front needle, and then (knit next st from back needle together with the next st from front needle) twice; rep from * to end. 136 (152, 168, 184) sts

BODY

To set up the Body, work two rounds of stockinette stitch (knit every stitch). Then:

Rnds 1, 2, 3, and 4: Knit every stitch.

At the end of the fourth round, remove the marker, slip 2 sts purlwise, replace marker (start of round has now moved forward by 2 sts).

Rnd 5: *(Pick up one stitch from the WS five rounds down and knit it together with next stitch) three times, k5; rep from * to end.

Note: When picking up the stitch on the WS, do this in the same way that you did the tucks. This helps keep the Body tucks consistent with the Brim tucks. Because there are only four plain rounds worked between picking up and creating the tucks, the first stitch of each tuck will be from the join round in the previous tuck.

Repeat these five rounds until work measures approximately 5.5 (6.5, 7.5, 8.5) in./14 (16.5, 19, 21.5) cm from Brim edge, ending after a Rnd 5.

CROWN

To set up for the Crown, work one round of stockinette stitch (knit every stitch).

Rnd 1: *K1, k2tog; rep from * to last 1 (2, 0, 1) sts, k1 (2, 0, 1). 91 (102, 112, 123) sts

Work a further four rounds of stockinette stitch and repeat the tuck-making process used in the Brim by picking up the stitches from the purl bumps on the reverse of the decrease round.

Rnd 2: *K1, k2tog; rep from * to last 1 (0, 1, 0) sts, k1 (0, 1, 0). 61 (68, 75, 82) sts

Work a further four rounds of stockinette stitch and repeat the tuck-making process by picking up the stitches from the purl bumps on the reverse of the decrease round.

Rnd 3: *K1, k2tog; rep from * to last 1 (2, 0, 1) sts, k1 (2, 0, 1). 41 (46, 50, 55) sts

Work a further four rounds of stockinette stitch and repeat the tuck-making process by picking up the stitches from the purl bumps on the reverse of the decrease round.

Rnd 4: *K2tog; rep from * to last 1 (0, 0, 1) sts, k1 (0, 0, 1). 21 (23, 25, 28) sts

Work a further four rounds of stockinette stitch and repeat the tuck-making process by picking up the stitches from the purl bumps on the reverse of the decrease round.

Rnd 5: *K2tog; rep from * to last 1 (1, 1, 0) sts, k1 (1, 1, 0). 11 (12, 13, 14) sts

Break yarn and draw through remaining 11 (12, 13, 14) sts; tighten to close.

FINISHING

Weave in all ends. A gentle wash and blocking are required to help the tucks and decreases settle.

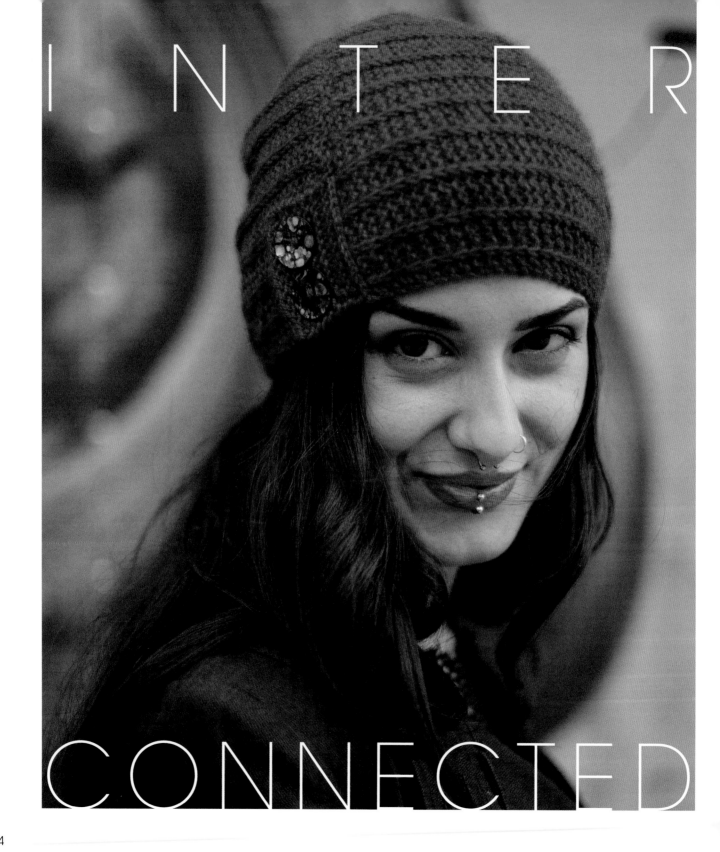

INTER

CONNECTED

SIZES

Note: Size changes are made by adjusting needle size.

To fit size: 21 in./53.25 cm, use US 5 (3.75 mm) needles

Finished size: Circumference, 16.75 in./42.5 cm; Length, 9.75 in./24.75 cm

To fit size: 23 in./58.5 cm, use US 6 (4 mm) needles

Finished size: Circumference, 18.75 in./47.75 cm; Length, 10.75 in./27.5 cm

YARN

127 (152) yd./116 (139) m worsted weight (medium), plied yarn

Additional 51 yd./47 m for a 6 × 6 in./15 × 15 cm swatch in garter st

NEEDLES & NOTIONS

Pair US 5 (US 6)/3.75 mm (4 mm) straight needles (or size needed to obtain gauge)

US 8 (5 mm) needle for bind-off

US G-6 (4 mm) crochet hook

Approx. 2 yd./2 m waste yarn

Tapestry needle

Two 7/8 in. (2.25 cm) coordinating buttons

SAMPLE DETAILS

Shown in Neighborhood Fiber Company Cobblestone Worsted (200 yd./183 m per 4 oz./114 g; 75% bluefaced Leicester wool, 15% cashmere, 10% silk)

Shown in size 21 in./53.25 cm on model with 21.25 in./54 cm circumference head

GAUGE

To fit size: 21 in./53.25 cm

Gauge: With US 5 (3.75 mm) needles, 20 sts × 40 rows to 4 in./10 cm over pattern; 19 sts × 38 rows to 4 in./10 cm over garter st

To fit size: 23 in./58.5 cm

Gauge: With US 6 (4 mm) needles, 18 sts × 36 rows to 4 in./10 cm over pattern; 17 sts × 34 rows to 4 in./10 cm over garter st

CHARTS

Page 128

SKILLS REQUIRED

- knit and purl stitches
- slipped stitches
- short rows (see page 122)
- provisional cast-on (see page 124)
- grafting (see page 120)

HINTS

With this pattern, row gauge is the important factor, as this affects the fit around the body, and the stitch gauge affects the depth of the hat. The pattern is constructed of panels that are worked consecutively, and each panel starts on a wrong side row. You will work Panel 1 three times, Panel 2 three times, Panel 1 three times, and, finally, Panel 2 three times. You can also mix and match these panels to create your own interconnected pattern, ensuring that a total of 12 panels are worked.

SPECIAL STITCHES/ABBREVIATIONS

SR = Short row; wrap and turn (w&t) or, with the German short row method, work the double stitch here. To work a wrap and turn, bring the working yarn to the front between the needles, slip the next stitch purlwise, bring the yarn back between the needles, and slip the stitch back to the left-hand needle (stitch wrapped); turn. On the next row, work the wrap and stitch together as one. To work the German short rows, see page 122.

INSTRUCTIONS

Using waste yarn and provisional cast-on method and using US 5 (US 6) needles, cast on 49 sts. Change to main yarn and work panel as follows:

PANEL 1 (Refer to Chart 1)

Row 1 (WS): K1, (sl 1, k3) 12 times.
Row 2 (RS): K47, SR.
Row 3: K3, (sl 1, k3) 11 times.
Row 4 and all even rows: Knit to 2 sts before last short row stitch, SR.
Row 5: K1, (sl 1, k3) 9 times, sl 1, SR.
Row 7: K3, (sl 1, k3) 10 times.
Row 9: K1, (sl 1, k3) 10 times.
Row 11: K3, (sl 1, k3) 9 times.
Row 13: K1, (sl 1, k3) 7 times, sl 1, SR.
Row 15: K3, (sl 1, k3) 8 times.
Row 17: K1, (sl 1, k3) 8 times.
Row 18: Knit across all sts, working the short rows as you go. Repeat these 18 rows 3 times in total, and then proceed to Panel 2.

PANEL 2 (Refer to Chart 2)

Row 1 (WS): K3, (sl 1, k3) 11 times, sl 1, k1.
Row 2 (RS): K47, SR.
Row 3: K1, (sl 1, k3) 11 times, sl 1, k1.
Row 4 and all even rows: Knit to 2 sts before last short row stitch, SR.
Row 5: K3, (sl 1, k3) 8 times, sl 1, k2, SR.
Row 7: K1, (sl 1, k3) 10 times, sl 1, k1.
Row 9: K3, (sl 1, k3) 9 times, sl 1, k1.
Row 11: K1, (sl 1, k3) 9 times, sl 1, k1.
Row 13: K3, (sl 1, k3) 6 times, sl 1, k2, SR.
Row 15: K1, (sl 1, k3) 8 times, sl 1, k1.
Row 17: K3, (sl 1, k3) 7 times, sl 1, k1.
Row 18: Knit across all sts, working the short rows as you go.

Repeat these 18 rows three times in total, then proceed to Panel 1 three more times, and then work Panel 2 a final three times.

On the final (12th) panel, omit the last row and work as follows:

Prep row: With a larger needle, loosely bind off 16 sts; hold remaining stitches for the graft.

JOINING THE PANELS (Grafting)

Carefully remove the provisional cast-on stitch by stitch, transferring the live stitches to 2nd needle and repositioning them as necessary. You will graft with the working yarn; cut the working yarn, leaving a 1 yd./1 m tail.

Slip the first 16 sts from the Brim edge of the released stitches to a spare needle or waste yarn—these will be worked for the button tab.

When grafting across short rows, you will treat the short rows in exactly the same way that you have throughout the pattern. If you knitted across the wraps, you can ignore them when grafting.

If you worked wrap and turn (w&t) short rows and picked up the wrap (from the RS) and then worked into the back of the stitch+wrap previously, you will need to do the same for the graft. To do this, lift both the wrap and the stitch off and twist toward you, and then place these back on the needle and perform garter st Kitchener as normal. If you worked into the front of the stitch+wrap previously, you do not need to twist them during the graft. If you worked German short rows, then treat the double-leg stitch as one stitch when grafting, just as you did when knitting.

You will be grafting from the end of the button tab up. Once the graft is complete, thread yarn through edge stitches and pull to tighten to close the crown.

BUTTON TAB

With RS facing and using larger needle, loosely bind off 16 sts.

With WS facing and using US 5 (US 6) needles, pick up 16 sts from the back of the bind-off.

Row 1: K4, k2tog, k4, k2tog, k4. (14 sts)

Now work 15 rows of garter st (knit every stitch).

With RS facing and using larger needle, loosely bind off all sts.

FINISHING

Weave in all ends and block as required. Sew down buttons in position as shown.

AZULA

SIZES

Note: Sizing in this pattern is achieved through adjusting needle size. The sideways nature of this design creates a great deal of stretch, so do consider the negative ease.

To fit size: 20 in./51 cm, use US 3 (3.25 mm) needles

Finished sizes: Circumference, 16 in./40.75 cm; Length, 8.9 in./22.5 cm

To fit size: 22 in./56 cm, use US 4 (3.5 mm) needles

Finished sizes: Circumference, 17.4 in./44.25 cm; Length, 9.6 in./24.5 cm

YARN

Yarn A: 105 yd./95 m DK weight (light), plied yarn

Yarn B: 158 yd./144 m DK weight (light), plied yarn

Additional 61 yd./56 m for a 6 × 6 in./15 × 15 cm swatch in garter st

NEEDLES & NOTIONS

Pair US 3 (US 4)/3.25 mm (3.5 mm) straight needles (or size needed to obtain gauge)

US D-3 (3.25 mm) crochet hook

Approx. 3 yd./3 m waste yarn

Tapestry needle

SAMPLE DETAILS

Shown in The Yarn Collective Bloomsbury DK (263 yd./240 m per 3.5 oz./100 g; 100% merino)

Shown in size 20 in./51 cm on model with 19.5 in./49.5 cm circumference head

GAUGE

To fit size: 20 in./51 cm

Gauge: With US 3 (3.25 mm) needles, 24 sts × 48 rows to 4 in./10 cm over garter st

To fit size: 22 in./56 cm

Gauge: With US 4 (3.5 mm) needles, 22 sts × 44 rows to 4 in./10 cm over garter st

SKILLS REQUIRED

- knit and purl stitches
- short rows (see page 122)
- provisional cast-on (see page 124)
- two-color Kitchener stitch grafting in garter stitch (see page 126)

HINTS

With this pattern, row gauge is the important factor, as this affects the fit around the body, while the stitch gauge affects the depth of the hat.

The pattern is constructed of panels that are worked consecutively, and each panel starts on a wrong side row. You will work the panel eight times in total.

Yarn A is used for the background color, Yarn B for the flames. You will occasionally need to carry Yarn B across the back of the work—technically upward, between rows; to help keep an even tension and avoid snags, the yarn can be held behind Yarn A. To change colors, simply swap the yarns over on the wrong side of the work, ensuring that the yarns cross to avoid holes where the colors change.

The recommended short row method is German short rows, as these are easy to manage within garter stitch, are double sided, and are easily graftable (you simply treat the double stitch as a normal stitch, just as you do when knitting over them). You can, of course, use any short row method, but do consider how it looks from both sides (as the short rows traverse) and how easy they are to graft (there are only a few short row stitches that will require grafting to finish the hat).

CHART

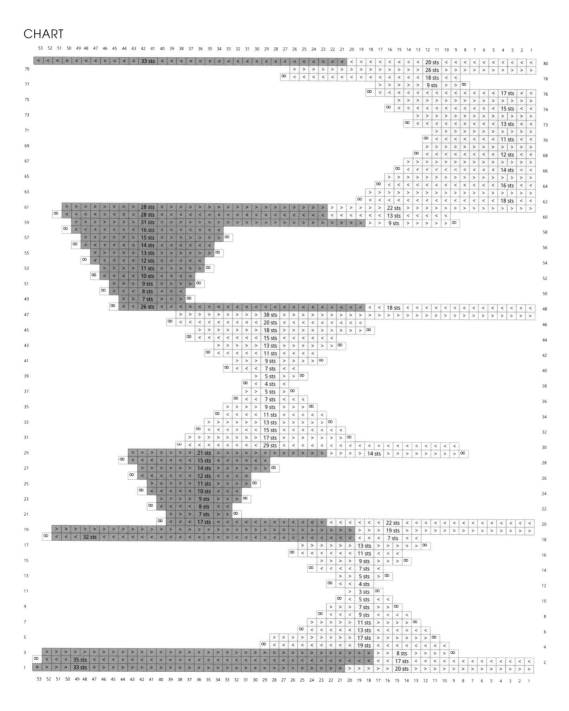

KEY

> = Yarn A, knit on WS.

< = Yarn A, knit on RS.

> = Yarn B, knit on WS.

< = Yarn B, knit on RS.

∞ = Work short row (SR). For the wrap and turn (w&t) method, this is the stitch that is wrapped. For the German short row method, this is the double-leg stitch.

INSTRUCTIONS

Using waste yarn and provisional cast-on method, cast on 53 sts. Change to main yarn and work panel as directed in the chart map.

Repeat these 80 rows eight times in total. On the final repeat, omit final row, as this will be replaced by Kitchener grafting.

FINISHING

Carefully remove provisional cast-on stitch by stitch, taking care to keep in pattern, transferring live stitches to second needle. You'll graft with the working yarn; cut the working yarn, leaving a 1 yd./1 m tail.

Bring both sets of stitches together and perform Kitchener stitch for garter stitch across all the stitches. When grafting across short rows, you will treat the short rows in exactly the same way that you have throughout the pattern. If you knitted across the short rows, you can treat them as a regular stitch when grafting.

To graft across the color change between Yarn A and Yarn B, simply work the first stitch on each needle with Yarn A and the second stitch with Yarn B—this effectively closes off the first yarn and begins again with the second. To create a clean graft in garter stitch, you need to bring an odd number of rows together—hence the final row on the final panel isn't knitted and will be replaced by the graft. You will be grafting from the bottom of the hat up. Once the graft is complete, thread yarn through the edge stitches and pull to tighten to close the crown. Weave in all ends and block as required.

KLASTAR

SIZES

To fit sizes: 20 (22, 24) in./51 (56, 61) cm

Finished sizes: 16 (18, 20) in./40.5 (45.75, 51) cm

YARN

Yarn A: 178 (201, 223) yd./163 (183, 204) m DK weight (light), plied yarn

Yarn B: 134 (150, 167) yd./122 (137, 153) m DK weight (light), plied yarn

Additional 46 yd./42 m for a 6 × 6 in./15 × 15 cm swatch in garter st

NEEDLES & NOTIONS

Pair US 3 (3.25 mm) straight needles (or size needed to obtain gauge)

US E-4 (3.5 mm) crochet hook

Approx. 2 yd./2 m waste yarn

Stitch marker as necessary

Tapestry needle

SAMPLE DETAILS

Shown in Indigo Dragonfly DK Matter (280 yd./256 m per 3.5 oz./100 g; 100% superwash merino) and Hand Dyed by Kate Smooth Merino DK (274 yd./250 m per 3.5 oz./100 g; 100% superwash merino)

Shown in size 20 in./51 cm on model with 21 in./53.25 cm circumference head

GAUGE

Note: Fit is determined by row gauge; if your gauge differs, simply work more or fewer panels to achieve the desired size. Additional notes on adjustment are included.

24 sts × 48 rows to 4 in./10 cm on US 3 (3.25 mm) needles over garter st

30 sts × 36 rows to 4 in./10 cm on US 3 (3.25 mm) needles over garter st–based pattern

CHART

Page 129

HINTS

Row gauge determines how well the hat fits. The garter stitch is designed to work as ribbing for the brim and should be measured relaxed.

As this pattern is based on garter stitch, the wraps from the short rows do not need to be picked up when working across them—they will remain fairly well hidden in the stitch pattern.

This pattern consists of a series of panels, knitted sideways consecutively. The width of each panel is 2 in./5 cm when row gauge is met. You can adjust the number of panels to your liking.

Adjusting the depth and slouch of the hat is managed by changing gauge or by adding or removing repeats shown at the adjustment point on the chart.

Yarn A is used for the background color, Yarn B for the clusters. You will occasionally need to carry either yarn across the back of the work—technically upward, between rows. To help keep an even tension and avoid snags, the dormant yarn can be held behind the active yarn. To change colors, simply swap the yarns over on the WS of the work, ensuring that the yarns cross to avoid holes where the colors change. Should you wish, the yarn floats and changes can be made on the RS for an alternative finish. Alternatively, if you break the yarn that would be carried and carefully weave in the ends, you can make your hat fully reversible.

SKILLS REQUIRED

- knit and purl stitches
- yarn overs
- cluster stitches
- short rows (see page 122)
- provisional cast-on (see page 124)
- grafting/Kitchener stitch (see page 120)

SPECIAL STITCHES/ABBREVIATIONS

(A) = Work with Yarn A.

(B) = Work with Yarn B.

SR = Work short row. For the wrap and turn (w&t) method, this is the stitch that is wrapped. For the German short row method, this is the double-legged stitch. To work a wrap and turn, bring the working yarn to the front between the needles, slip the next stitch purlwise, bring the yarn back between the needles, and slip the stitch back to the left-hand needle (stitch wrapped); turn. On the next row, work the wrap and stitch together as one. To work the German short rows, see page 122.

MK = Slip 5 sts to right-hand needle, dropping extra loops; slip these 5 sts back to left-hand needle, and then (k1, yo, k1, yo, k1) into all 5 sts together through the backs of the loops.

INSTRUCTIONS

Using waste yarn and provisional cast-on method, cast on 66 sts. Change to main yarn and work panel as follows (see chart):

Row 1 (WS): With Yarn A, knit to end.

Row 2 (RS): (A) k10, (B) ((k1, yo) 5 times, sl 1) 9 times, SR.

Row 3: (B) (sl 1, MK) 9 times, (A) k10.

Row 4: (A) k63, SR.

Row 5: (A) knit to end.

Row 6: (A) k13, (B) ((k1, yo) 5 times, sl 1) 8 times, SR.

Row 7: (B) (sl 1, MK) 8 times, (A) k13.

Row 8: (A) k59, SR.

Row 9: (A) knit to end.

Row 10: (A) k10, (B) ((k1, yo) 5 times, sl 1) 8 times, SR.

Row 11: (B) (sl 1, MK) 8 times, (A) k10.

Row 12: (A) k65, SR.

Row 13: (A) knit to end.

Row 14: (A) k13, (B) ((k1, yo) 5 times, sl 1) 7 times, SR.

Row 15: (B) (sl 1, MK) 7 times, (A) k13.

Row 16: (A) k54, SR.

Row 17: (A) knit to end.

Row 18: (A) k10, (B) ((k1, yo) 5 times, sl 1) 8 times, SR.

Row 19: (B) (sl 1, MK) 8 times, (A) k10.

Row 20: (A) k57, SR.

Row 21: (A) knit to end.

Row 22: (A) k13, (B) ((k1, yo) 5 times, sl 1) 8 times, SR.

Row 23: (B) (sl 1, MK) 8 times, (A) k13.

Row 24: (A) knit across all sts working the short rows as you go.

Repeat these 24 rows 8 (9, 10) times in total. On the final repeat, omit final row, as this will be replaced by the Kitchener grafting.

FINISHING

Carefully remove provisional cast-on stitch by stitch, taking care to keep in pattern, transferring live stitches to second needle. You will graft with the working yarn; cut the working yarn, leaving a 1 yd./1 m tail.

Bring both sets of stitches together and perform Kitchener stitch for garter stitch across all the stitches. When grafting across short rows, you will treat the short rows in exactly the same way that you have throughout the pattern. If you knitted across the short rows, you can treat them as a regular stitch when grafting.

To create a clean graft in garter stitch, you need to bring an odd number of rows together—hence the final row on the final panel isn't knitted, and it will be replaced by the graft. You will be grafting from the bottom of the hat up. Once the graft is complete, thread yarn through the edge stitches and pull to tighten to close the crown.

Weave in all ends and block as required.

JOYCE

SIZES

To fit size: 17 (19, 21, 23) in./43.25 (48.25, 53.25, 58.5) cm

Finished size: 15 (16.75, 18.25, 20) in./38 (42.5, 46.25, 51) cm

YARN

Yarn A: 89 (100, 137, 154) yd./81 (91, 125, 141) m sport weight (fine), plied yarn

Yarn B: 66 (74.3, 103, 128) yd./60 (68, 94, 117) m sport weight (fine), plied yarn

66 yd./60 m for the pom-pom (optional)

Additional 54 yd./49 m for a 6 × 6 in./15 × 15 cm swatch in garter st

NEEDLES & NOTIONS

Pair US 3 (3.25 mm) straight needles (or size needed to obtain gauge)

US D-3 (3.25 mm) crochet hook

Cable needle

Stitch marker as necessary

Tapestry needle

SAMPLE DETAILS

Shown in Stolen Stitches Nua (153 yd./140 m per 1.75 oz./50 g; 60% merino, 20% yak, 20% linen)

Shown in size 21 in./53.25 cm on model with 22 in./56 cm circumference head

GAUGE

24 sts × 48 rows to 4 in./10 cm on US 3 (3.25 mm) needles over garter st

24 sts × 56 rows to 4 in./10 cm on US 3 (3.25 mm) needles over slipped stitch pattern

SKILLS REQUIRED

- knit and purl stitches
- increases and decreases
- special cast-on (see pattern instructions)
- twisted stitches
- pom-poms

H I N T

Stitches are slipped purlwise.

SPECIAL STITCHES/ABBREVIATIONS

C2B = Slip next st onto cable needle and hold at back of work, knit next st, and then knit the st from the cable needle.

C2F = Slip next st onto cable needle and hold at front of work, knit next st, and then knit the st from the cable needle.

INSTRUCTIONS

Using crochet provisional cast-on method as a permanent cast-on, and using Yarn A, cast on 90 (100, 110, 120) sts.

Knit all sts, working one row flat, and then join in the round, being careful not to twist sts. Place stitch marker to indicate start of round.

BRIM

Rnd 1: Purl all sts.
Rnd 2: Knit all sts.

Repeat these two rounds, creating garter st in the round, until work measures approx. 1 (1, 1.25, 1.25) in./2.5 (2.5, 3.25, 3.25) cm, ending after a Rnd 1, and then work increase round once as follows:

Inc rnd: *K5, M1; rep from * to end. 108 (120, 132, 144) sts

BODY, PART 1 (Refer to Chart 1)

From this point onward, all even rounds are worked with Yarn A and all odd rounds are worked with Yarn B.

Rnd 1: With Yarn B, *p5, sl 1; rep from * to end.
Rnd 2: With Yarn A, knit all sts.

Sizes 17 in./43.25 cm and 19 in./48.25 cm continue at Rnd 5.

Rnd 3: *P5, sl 1; rep from * to end.
Rnd 4: Knit all sts.
Rnd 5: *P5, sl 1; rep from * to end.
Rnd 6: *K4, C2B, k6; rep from * to end.
Rnd 7: *P4, sl 2, p5, sl 1; rep from * to end.

Rnd 8: *K3, C2B, C2F, k5; rep from * to end.
Rnd 9: *P3, sl 1, p2, sl 1, p4, sl 1; rep from * to end.
Rnd 10: Knit all sts.
Rnd 11: *P3, sl 1, p2, sl 1, p4, sl 1; rep from * to end.
Rnd 12: *K3, C2F, C2B, k5; rep from * to end.
Rnd 13: *P4, sl 2, p5, sl 1; rep from * to end.
Rnd 14: *K4, C2F, k6; rep from * to end.
Rnd 15: *P5, sl 1; rep from * to end.
Rnd 16: Knit all sts.

Sizes 17 in./43.25 cm and 19 in./48.25 cm continue at Rnd 19.

Rnd 17: *P5, sl 1; rep from * to end.
Rnd 18: Knit all sts.
Rnd 19: *P5, sl 1; rep from * to end.
Rnd 20: *K10, C2B; rep from * to end.
Rnd 21: *P5, sl 1, p4, sl 2; rep from * to end; RM, slip stitch, PM.
Rnd 22: *K8, C2B, C2F; rep from * to end.
Rnd 23: *P4, sl 1, p3, sl 1, p2, sl 1; rep from * to end.
Rnd 24: Knit all sts.
Rnd 25: *P4, sl 1, p3, sl 1, p2, sl 1; rep from * to end.
Rnd 26: *K8, C2F, C2B; rep from * to end.

You will now need to move the stitch marker back to the original start-of-round point—RM, unpick second stitch of the last C2B of the previous round and place stitch on the left-hand needle; PM.

Rnd 27: *P5, sl 1, p4, sl 2; rep from * to end.
Rnd 28: *K10, C2F; rep from * to end.

BODY, PART 2 (Refer to Chart 2)

Rnds 29 to 42: Work as Rnds 1 to 14.

Rnd 43: *P11, sl 1; rep from * to end.

Rnd 44: Knit all sts.

Sizes 17 in./43.25 cm and 19 in./48.25 cm continue at Rnd 47.

Rnd 45: *P11, sl 1; rep from * to end.

Rnd 46: Knit all sts.

Rnd 47: *P11, sl 1; rep from * to end.

Rnd 48: *K10, C2B; rep from * to end.

Rnd 49: *P10, sl 2; rep from * to end; RM, slip stitch, PM.

Rnd 50: *K8, C2B, C2F; rep from * to end.

Rnd 51: *P8, sl 1, p2, sl 1; rep from * to end.

Rnd 52: Knit all sts.

Rnd 53: *P8, sl 1, p2, sl 1; rep from * to end.

Rnd 54: *K8, C2F, C2B; rep from * to end.

You will now need to move the stitch marker back to the original start-of-round point—RM, unpick second stitch of the last C2B of the previous round and place stitch on the left-hand needle; PM.

Rnd 55: *P10, sl 2; rep from * to end.

Rnd 56: *K10, C2F; rep from * to end.

Rnd 57: Purl all sts.

Rnd 58: Knit all sts.

Repeat these last two rounds until work measures approx. 4.5 (5, 5.75, 6.5) in./11.5 (12.75, 14.5, 16.5) cm from the cast-on edge, ending after a Rnd 58.

Crown prep rnd: *P18 (20, 22, 24), PM; rep from * to end.

CHART 1

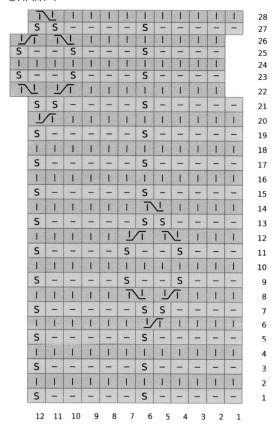

CHART 2

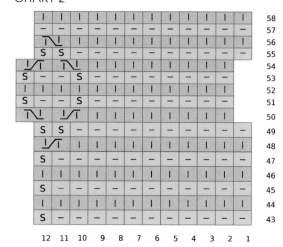

KEY

▨ = Work with Yarn A.

☐ = Work with Yarn B.

☐ I = Knit.

☐ − = Purl.

S = Slip 1 st purlwise.

◣ = C2B. Slip next st onto cable needle and hold at back of work, knit next st, and then knit the st from the cable needle.

◢ = C2F. Slip next st onto cable needle and hold at front of work, knit next st, and then knit the st from the cable needle.

CROWN

Rnd 1: *Knit to 2 sts before marker, k2tog; rep from * to end. (decreases 6 sts per round)

Rnd 2: Purl all sts.

Repeat these two rounds until 54 (60, 66, 72) sts remain, ending after a Rnd 2.

Rnd 3: *Knit to 2 sts before marker, k2tog; rep from * to end.

Rnd 4: *Purl to 1 st before marker, sl 1; rep from * to end.

Repeat these two rounds until a total of 12 sts remain, ending after a Rnd 2.

Break yarn and draw through remaining 12 sts; tighten to close.

POM-POM

Cut 2 circular pieces measuring 3 in./7.5 cm diameter from thin cardboard. The inner circle should be approximately 1.5 in./3.75 cm. Placing the two pieces of cardboard together, wrap the yarn through the center and around the outer circle, continuing in this manner until the entire piece of cardboard is covered. Continue wrapping the yarn until either the center hole has closed or all the yarn has been used.

Carefully cut the yarn along the edge of the circle to reveal the covered cardboard. Cut all of the yarn, and then tie a knot between the two layers of cardboard, effectively tying all the pieces of yarn together, before removing the cardboard. Trim pom-pom before attaching securely to the hat.

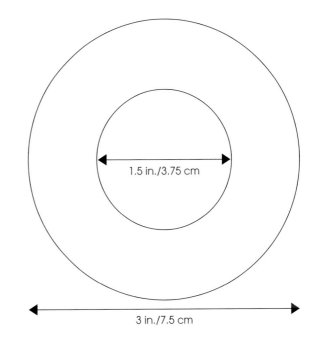

FINISHING

Weave in all ends. A gentle wash and blocking are required to help the decrease lines settle and lay flat.

SCOURIE

SIZES

To fit size: 19 (21, 23) in./48.25 (53.25, 58.5) cm

Finished size: 16 (18, 20) in./40.75 (45.75, 51) cm

YARN

Yarn A: 197 (222, 247) yd./181 (203, 226) m sport weight (fine), plied yarn

Yarn B: 42.6 (47, 53) yd./39 (43, 48) m sport weight (fine), plied yarn

Additional 50 yd./46 m for a 6 × 6 in./15 × 15 cm swatch in garter st

NEEDLES & NOTIONS

Pair US 2½ (3 mm) straight needles (or size needed to obtain gauge)

US C-2 or D-3 (3 mm) crochet hook

Approx. 3 yd./3 m waste yarn

Tapestry needle

SAMPLE DETAILS

Shown in Ripples Crafts Merino Sport Weight (286 yd./262 m per 3.5 oz./100 g; 100% merino)

Shown in size 21 in./53.25 cm on model with 21.75 in./55.25 cm circumference head

GAUGE

24 sts × 48 rows to 4 in./10 cm on US 2½ (3 mm) needles over garter st

SKILLS REQUIRED

- knit and purl stitches
- short rows (see page 122)
- provisional cast-on (see page 124)
- grafting (see page 120)

HINTS

With this pattern, row gauge is the important factor, as this affects the fit around the body, and the stitch gauge affects the depth of the hat.

The pattern is constructed of panels that are worked consecutively, and each panel starts on a wrong side row. You will work the panel 8 (9, 10) times in total.

Yarn A is used for the background color, Yarn B for the ovals. You will occasionally need to carry either yarn across the back of the work—technically upward, between rows. To help keep an even tension and avoid snags, the yarn can be held behind the other yarn. To change colors, simply swap the yarns over on the wrong side of the work, ensuring that the yarns cross to avoid holes where the colors change.

The recommended short row method is German short rows, as these are easy to manage within garter stitch, are double sided, and are easily graftable (simply treat the double stitch as a normal stitch, just as you do when knitting over them). You can, of course, use any short row method, but do consider how it looks from both sides (as the short rows traverse) and how easy they are to graft (there are only a few short row stitches that will require grafting to finish).

CHART

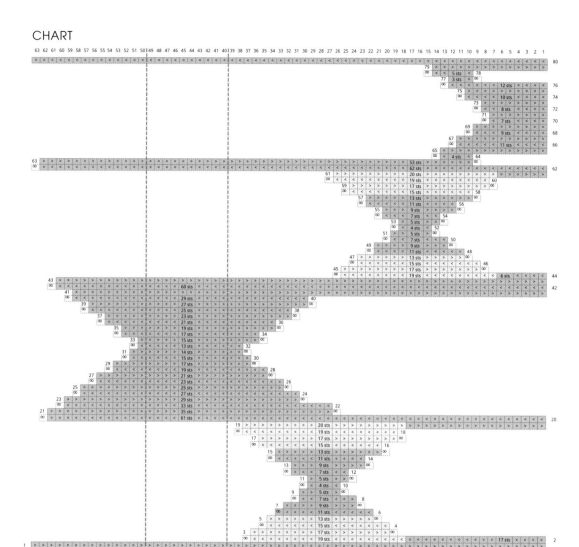

KEY

> = With Yarn A, knit on WS.

< = With Yarn A, knit on RS.

> = With Yarn B, knit on WS.

< = With Yarn B, knit on RS.

∞ = Work short row. For the German short row method, this is the double-leg stitch. For the wrap and turn method, this is the stitch that is wrapped.

<< adjustment points >>

Note about the knitting chart: The hat is worked in garter stitch throughout. Stitch counts are provided to help you keep track of the short rows more easily. Turning stitches are not included in the listed stitch counts. For additional orientation, the direction of work is marked with > and < symbols.

This hat has been carefully engineered to provide a balanced fabric, incorporating brim and crown shaping. Any adjustments or amendments to the placement of the short rows may cause the knitted fabric to become distorted and result in unflattering changes in the overall shape of the hat. To alter the length to compensate for gauge or taste, stitches should be added or removed between the marked adjustment points only.

INSTRUCTIONS

Using waste yarn and provisional cast-on method, cast on 63 sts. Change to main yarn and work panel as directed in the chart.

Repeat these 80 rows 8 (9, 10) times in total. On the final repeat, omit final row, as this will be replaced by Kitchener grafting.

FINISHING

Carefully remove provisional cast-on stitch by stitch, taking care to keep in pattern, transferring live stitches to second needle. You will graft with the working yarn; cut the working yarn, leaving a 1 yd./1 m tail.

Bring both sets of stitches together and perform Kitchener stitch for garter stitch across all the stitches. When grafting across short rows, you will treat the short rows in exactly the same way that you have throughout the pattern. If you knitted across the short rows, you can treat them as a regular stitch when grafting.

To create a clean graft in garter stitch, you need to bring an odd number of rows together—hence the final row on the final panel isn't knitted and will be replaced by the graft. You will be grafting from the bottom of the hat up. Once the graft is complete, thread yarn through the edge stitches and pull to close the crown.

Weave in all ends and block as required.

CORELLA

SIZES

To fit size: 19 (21, 23) in./48.25 (53.25, 58.5) cm

Finished size: 16.5 (18.5, 20.25) in./42 (47, 51.5) cm

YARN

154 (171, 227.5) yd./141 (156, 208) m sport weight (fine), plied yarn

Additional 29 yd./26 m for a 6 × 6 in./15 × 15 cm swatch in St st

NEEDLES & NOTIONS

Set each of US 2½ (3 mm) and US 3 (3.25 mm) DPNs or circular needles (or size needed to obtain gauge)

Stitch marker as necessary

Tapestry needle

SAMPLE DETAILS

Shown in Shibui Knits Baby Alpaca (255 yd./233 m per 3.5 oz./100 g; 100% alpaca)

Shown in size 21 in./53.25 cm on model with 21.75 in./55.25 cm circumference head

Alternative yarn: Frog Tree Alpaca Sportweight (130 yd./119 m per 1.75 oz./50 g; 100% alpaca)

GAUGE

24 sts × 30 rows to 4 in./10 cm on US 3 (3.25 mm) needles over St st

26 sts × 40 rows to 4 in./10 cm on US 2½ (3 mm) needles over twisted rib, lightly stretched

SKILLS REQUIRED

- knit and purl stitches
- knitting in the round
- increases and decreases
- alternating rib cable cast-on
- knitting lace

SPECIAL STITCHES/ABBREVIATIONS

C4B = slip next 2 sts onto cable needle and hold at back, knit next 2 sts, and then knit the 2 sts from the cable needle (right cross).

C4F = slip next 2 sts onto cable needle and hold at front, knit next 2 sts, and then knit the 2 sts from the cable needle (left cross).

M1P = Pick up the horizontal loop between sts, place it onto the left needle, and then purl into the back of it.

I N S T R U C T I O N S

Using US 2½ needles and the alternating rib cable cast-on method (alternate casting on 1 knit and then 1 purl stitch), cast on 108 (120, 132) sts. Join in the round, being careful not to twist sts. Place stitch marker to indicate start of round.

BRIM

Now work twisted rib (k1tbl, p1) for 1 (1.25, 1.5) in./2.5 (3.25, 3.75) cm (or desired length), and then work increase round once as follows:

Inc rnd: *K1, M1, p1, k1, p1, M1, k1, p1, M1P; rep from * to end. 162 (180, 198) sts

BODY (Refer to Chart 1)

Change to US 3 needles and proceed as follows:

19 in./48.25 cm size: Work Rnds 1–32 once.
21 in./53.25 cm size: Work Rnds 1–32 once.
23 in./58.5 cm size: Work Rnds 16–32 and then Rnds 1–32 once.

Rnd 1: *Ssk, k2, p2, k1, yo, p2, yo, k1, p2, k2, k2tog, p2; rep from * to end.
Rnd 2: *K3, (p2, k2) twice, p2, k3, p2; rep from * to end.

Rnd 3: *Ssk, k1, p2, k1, yo, k1, p2, k1, yo, k1, p2, k1, k2tog, p2; rep from * to end.
Rnd 4: *K2, (p2, k3) twice, p2, k2, p2; rep from * to end.
Rnd 5: *Ssk, p2, k1, yo, k2, p2, k2, yo, k1, p2, k2tog, p2; rep from * to end.
Rnd 6: *K1, (p2, k4) twice, p2, k1, p2; rep from * to end.
Rnd 7: *Ssk, p1, k1, yo, k3, p2, k3, yo, k1, p1, k2tog, p2; rep from * to end.
Rnd 8: *K1, p1, k5, p2, k5, p1, k1, p2; rep from * to end.
Rnd 9: *Ssk, k1, yo, k4, p2, k4, yo, k1, k2tog, p2; rep from * to end.
Rnd 10: *K7, p2; rep from * to end.
Rnd 11: *Ssk, yo, p1, C4B, p2, C4F, p1, yo, k2tog, p2; rep from * to end.
Rnds 12, 13, and 14: *K1, (p2, k4) twice, p2, k1, p2; rep from * to end.
Rnd 15: *K1, p2, C4B, p2, C4F, p2, k1, p2; rep from * to end.
Rnd 16: *K1, (p2, k4) twice, p2, k1, p2; rep from * to end.
Rnd 17: *Yo, k1, p2, k2, k2tog, p2, ssk, k2, p2, k1, yo, p2; rep from * to end.
Rnd 18: *K2, (p2, k3) twice, p2, k2, p2; rep from * to end.
Rnd 19: *K1, yo, k1, p2, k1, k2tog, p2, ssk, k1, p2, k1, yo, k1, p2; rep from * to end.

Rnd 20: *K3, (p2, k2) twice, p2, k3, p2; rep from * to end.

Rnd 21: *K2, yo, k1, p2, k2tog, p2, ssk, p2, k1, yo, k2, p2; rep from * to end.

Rnd 22: *K4, (p2, k1) twice, p2, k4, p2; rep from * to end.

Rnd 23: *K3, yo, k1, p1, k2tog, p2, ssk, p1, k1, yo, k3, p2; rep from * to end.

Rnd 24: *K5, p1, k1, p2, k1, p1, k5, p2; rep from * to end.

Rnd 25: *K4, yo, k1, k2tog, p2, ssk, k1, yo, k4, p2; rep from * to end.

Rnd 26: *K7, p2; rep from * to end.

Rnd 27: *C4F, k1, yo, k2tog, p2, ssk, yo, k1, C4B, p2; rep from * to end.

Rnds 28, 29, and 30: *K4, (p2, k1) twice, p2, k4, p2; rep from * to end.

Rnd 31: *C4F, (p2, k1) twice, p2, C4B, p2; rep from * to end.

Rnd 32: *K4, (p2, k1) twice, p2, k4, p2; rep from * to end.

CHART 1

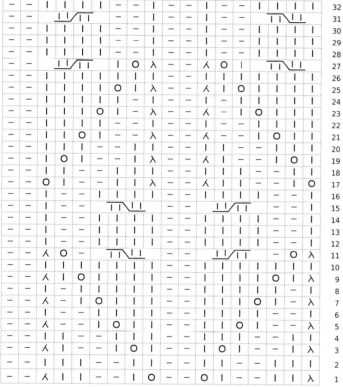

CHART 2

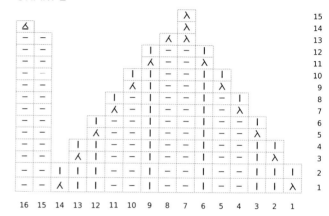

KEY

☐ | = Knit 1 stitch.

☐ − = Purl 1 stitch.

☐ O = Yarn over.

λ = Ssk. Slip next 2 sts knitwise, and then knit these 2 sts together through the backs of the loops.

∧ = Knit next 2 sts together.

◿ = Purl next 2 sts together.

⌐ I I／I I ⌐ = C4B. Slip next 2 sts onto cable needle and hold at back, knit next 2 sts, and then knit the 2 sts from the cable needle (right cross).

⌐ I I＼I I ⌐ = C4F. Slip next 2 sts onto cable needle and hold at front, knit next 2 sts, and then knit the 2 sts from the cable needle (left cross).

CROWN (Refer to Chart 2)

Rnd 1: *Ssk, k2, p2, (k1, p2) twice, k2, k2tog, p2; rep from * to end. 144 (160, 176) sts

Rnd 2: *K3, p2, (k1, p2) twice, k3, p2; rep from * to end.

Rnd 3: *Ssk, k1, p2, (k1, p2) twice, k1, k2tog, p2; rep from * to end. 126 (140, 154) sts

Rnd 4: *K2, p2, (k1, p2) twice, k2, p2; rep from * to end.

Rnd 5: *Ssk, p2, (k1, p2) twice, k2tog, p2; rep from * to end. 108 (120, 132) sts

Rnd 6: *K1, p2; rep from * to end.

Rnd 7: *Ssk, p1, k1, p2, k1, p1. k2tog, p2; rep from * to end. 90 (100, 110) sts

Rnd 8: *K1, p1, k1, p2; rep from * to end.

Rnd 9: *Ssk, k1, p2, k1, k2tog, p2; rep from * to end. 72 (80, 88) sts

Rnd 10: *K2, p2; rep from * to end.

Rnd 11: *Ssk, p2, k2tog, p2; rep from * to end. 54 (60, 66) sts

Rnd 12: *K1, p2; rep from * to end.

Rnd 13: *Ssk, k2tog, p2; rep from * to end. 36 (40, 44) sts

Rnd 14: *Ssk, p2tog; rep from * to end. 18 (20, 22) sts

Rnd 15: *Ssk; rep from * to end. 9 (10, 11) sts

Break yarn and draw through remaining 9 (10, 11) sts; tighten to close.

FINISHING

Weave in all ends. A gentle wash and blocking are recommended to help the stitches settle and lay flat. It is best to block this hat flat, as a circle with the crown at the center, to encourage the lace and cable pattern to open out. Avoid overstretching the brim during blocking, as doing so could cause your hat to become too big.

D U T R I E U

SIZES

To fit sizes: 20 (22) in./51 (56) cm

Finished size: 16.5 (18.5) in./42.25 (47) cm

YARN

164 (208) yd./150 (190) m 4-ply fingering or sock weight (super fine) yarn

Additional 50 yd./46 m for a 6 × 6 in./15 × 15 cm swatch in garter st

NEEDLES & NOTIONS

Pair of US 2 (2.75 mm) straight needles (or size needed to obtain gauge)

US C-2 (2.75 mm) crochet hook

Approx. 3 yd./3 m waste yarn

Hooked stitch marker or safety pin

Tapestry needle

1½ in. (3.75 cm) coordinating button

SAMPLE DETAILS

Shown in Cloudborn Fibers Highland Superwash Sock Twist Handpaints (178 yd./163 m per 1.75 oz./50 g; 80% merino, 20% nylon)

Shown in size 22 in./56 cm on model with 21.5 in./54.5 cm circumference head

GAUGE

27 sts × 38 rows to 4 in./10 cm on US 2 (2.75 mm) needles over St st

26 sts × 52 rows to 4 in./10 cm on US 2 (2.75 mm) needles over garter st

HINTS

This pattern consists of a series of panels, knitted sideways consecutively. There are six panels in total.

Row gauge determines how well the hat fits. The garter stitch is designed to work as ribbing and should be measured relaxed.

As this pattern is based on garter stitch, the wraps from the short rows do not need to be picked up when working across them should you prefer not to—they will remain fairly well hidden in the stitch pattern. Alternatively, you could use another preferred method for working the short rows.

Although only two sizes are included in this pattern due to the pattern constraints, you could adjust the gauge to create different sizes as required. Doing a gauge swatch would help you determine the finished size.

By all means adjust the increase ratio for a larger flap section, but be warned to not make it too big, as it will end up deeper than the Body section of the hat. Increasing every 10 rows/5 ridges on the 20 in./51 cm size creates a flap exactly the same depth as the Body section, for instance.

SKILLS REQUIRED

- knit and purl stitches
- increases and decreases
- short rows (see page 122)
- provisional cast-on (see page 124)
- grafting (see page 120)

SPECIAL STITCHES/ABBREVIATIONS

kfb = Knit into the front and back of the same stitch (increases 1 stitch).

w&t = Wrap and turn. Bring the working yarn to the front between the needles, slip the next stitch purlwise, bring the yarn back between the needles, and slip the stitch back to the left-hand needle (stitch wrapped); turn. On the next row, work the wrap and stitch together as one.

INSTRUCTIONS

Note: For both sizes, you will be increasing one stitch at Brim edge every 12 rows/6 ridges for the 20 in./51 cm size, and every 10 rows/5 ridges for the 22 in./56 cm size, and the first increase row will be Row 6.

You are advised to use a hooked stitch marker or safety pin to mark the last increase to help keep your increases evenly placed. Counting the ridges is the easiest way to keep track and ensure a smooth gradient.

Each increase row should be worked as follows:

Inc row: K1, kfb, knit to stitch before last wrapped stitch, w&t.

Using waste yarn and provisional cast-on method, cast on 40 (46) sts. Change to main yarn and work panel as follows:

Row 1 (WS): Knit all sts.

Row 2 (RS): Knit to last stitch, w&t.

Row 3: Knit all sts.

Row 4: Knit to stitch before last wrapped stitch, w&t.

Row 5: Knit all sts.

Repeat Rows 4 and 5 until 35 (39) rows have been worked, ending after a Row 5 (WS) row, and at the same time working the increases as directed throughout.

Next row: Knit across all sts.

Repeat these 36 (40) rows six times in total, continuing to increase 1st at the Brim edge as directed, giving you a final stitch count after 6 panels of 58 (70) sts.

On the final repeat and on the final row, do not knit across all the stitches; instead, bind off 18 (24) sts loosely, leaving 40 (46) sts on the needle for grafting.

FINISHING

Carefully remove provisional cast-on stitch by stitch, taking care to keep in pattern, transferring live stitches to second needle.

When grafting across short rows, you will treat the short rows in exactly the same way that you have throughout the pattern. If you knitted across the wraps, you can ignore them when grafting. If you picked up the wrap (from the RS) and then worked into the back of the stitch+wrap previously, you will need to do the same for the graft. To do this, lift both the wrap and the stitch off and twist toward you, and then place back on the needle and perform Kitchener stitch for garter stitch as normal (see page 120). If you worked into the front of the stitch+wrap previously, you do not need to twist them during the graft.

You will be grafting from the bottom of the hat up. Once the graft is complete, thread yarn through edge stitches and pull to tighten to close the crown.

Weave in all ends. Fold up flap and sew button in place. Blocking isn't necessary.

SKELTER

SIZES

To fit size: 17 (18.5, 20, 21.5, 23) in./43.25 (47, 51, 54.5, 58.5) cm

Finished size: 15.25 (16.5, 17.7, 19, 20.25) in./38.75 (42, 45, 48.25, 51.5) cm

YARN

88 (110, 128, 162, 188) yd./81 (101, 117, 148, 172) m worsted weight (medium), multi-plied yarn

63 yd./58 m for the pom-pom (optional; can also be a different yarn)

Additional 39 yd./36 m for a 6 × 6 in./15 × 15 cm swatch in garter st

NEEDLES & NOTIONS

Set of US 6 (4 mm) DPNs or circular needle (or size needed to obtain gauge)

Stitch marker as necessary

Tapestry needle

Cable needle

SAMPLE DETAILS

Shown in Rowan Pure Wool Worsted (219 yd./200 m per 3.5 oz./100 g; 100% wool)

Shown in size 21.5 in./54.5 cm on model with 21.75 in./55.25 cm circumference head

GAUGE

20 sts × 32 rows to 4 in./10 cm on US 6 (4 mm) needles over St st

19 sts × 38 rows to 4 in./10 cm on US 6 (4 mm) needles over garter st

SKILLS REQUIRED

- knit and purl stitches
- knitting in the round
- increases and decreases
- cables
- provisional cast-on (see page 124)
- pom-poms

SPECIAL STITCHES/ABBREVIATIONS

C2F = Slip next st onto cable needle and hold at front of work, knit next st, and then knit the st from the cable needle.

C3FD = Slip next st onto cable needle and hold at front, knit next 2 sts together, and then knit st from the cable needle (cross with decrease).

C3DF = Slip next st onto right-hand needle, slip next st onto cable needle and hold at front, slip st from right needle back to left and knit together with next st, and then knit st from cable needle (cross with decrease).

INSTRUCTIONS

Using provisional cast-on method as a permanent cast-on, cast on 72 (78, 84, 90, 96) sts.

BRIM

Work garter st flat (knit every stitch, every row) until Brim measures 1.5 (1.5, 2, 2, 2.25) in./3.75 (3.75, 5, 5, 5.75) cm, ending after a WS row (RS shows cast-on edge), and then work increase round once as follows:

Inc rnd: *P1, k1, M1, k2, M1, k1, p1; rep from * to end. 96 (104, 112, 120, 128) sts

Join in the round, being careful not to twist sts. Place stitch marker to indicate start of round.

BODY

Rnd 1: *P1, C2F, k4, p1; rep from * to end.
Rnd 2: *P1, k1, C2F, k3, p1; rep from * to end.
Rnd 3: *P1, k2, C2F, k2, p1; rep from * to end.
Rnd 4: *P1, k3, C2F, k1, p1; rep from * to end.
Rnd 5: *P1, k4, C2F, p1; rep from * to end.
Rnd 6: *P1, k5, k1tbl, p1; rep from * to end.
Repeat these 6 rounds until the Body measures 2.25 (3, 3, 3.75, 4.5) in./5.75 (7.5, 7.5, 9.5, 11.5) cm, excluding the Brim, ending after a Rnd 6.

CROWN

Rnd 1: *P1, C3FD, k3, p1; rep from * to end. 84 (91, 98, 105, 112) sts
Rnd 2: *P1, k1, C2F, k2, p1; rep from * to end.
Rnd 3: *P1, k2, C2F, k1, p1; rep from * to end.
Rnd 4: *P1, k2, C3DF, p1; rep from * to end. 72 (78, 84, 90, 96) sts
Rnd 5: *P1, k3, k1tbl, p1; rep from * to end.
Rnd 6: *P1, C2F, k2, p1; rep from * to end.
Rnd 7: *P1, k1, C3FD, p1; rep from * to end. 60 (65, 70, 75, 80) sts
Rnd 8: *P1, k2, k1tbl, p1; rep from * to end.
Rnd 9: *P1, C2F, k1, p1; rep from * to end.
Rnd 10: *P1, C3DF, p1; rep from * to end. 48 (52, 56, 60, 64) sts
Rnd 11: *P1, k1, k1tbl, p1; rep from * to end.
Rnd 12: *P1, C2F, p1; rep from * to end.
Rnd 13: *P1, ssk, p1; rep from * to end. 36 (39, 42, 45, 48) sts
Rnd 14: *P1, k1tbl, p1; rep from * to end, RM, p1, PM.
Rnd 15: *K1tbl, p2tog; rep from * to end. 24 (26, 28, 30, 32) sts
Rnd 16: *K1tbl, p1; rep from * to end.
Rnd 17: *Ssk; rep from * to end. 12 (13, 14, 15, 16) sts

Rnd 18: K0 (1, 0, 1, 0), *ssk; rep from * to end. 6 (7, 7, 8, 8) sts
Break yarn and draw through remaining 6 (7, 7, 8, 8) sts;
tighten to close.

POM-POM

Cut two circular pieces measuring 3 in./7.5 cm diameter
from thin cardboard. The inner circle should be approximately 1.5 in./3.75 cm (see illustration on page 31). Placing the two pieces of cardboard together, wrap the yarn
through the center and around the outer circle, continuing in this manner until all the cardboard is covered. Continue wrapping the yarn until either the center hole has
closed or all the yarn has been used.

Carefully cut the yarn along the edge of the circle to
reveal the covered cardboard. Cut all of the yarn, and
then tie a knot between the two layers of cardboard,
effectively tying all the pieces of yarn together, before
removing the cardboard. Trim pom-pom before attaching securely to the hat (it is advisable to block the hat
before attaching the pom-pom).

FINISHING

Weave in all ends. A gentle wash and blocking are required to help the decrease lines settle and lay flat.

FLORALYS

SIZES

To fit sizes: 18 (20, 22, 24) in./45.5 (51, 56, 61) cm

Finished size: 16 (18, 20, 22) in./40.5 (45.5, 51, 56) cm

YARN

140 (172, 208, 260) yd./128 (157, 190, 238) m heavy DK or worsted weight (medium), plied yarn

Additional 40 yd./37 m for a 6 × 6 in./15 × 15 cm swatch in St st

NEEDLES & NOTIONS

Set of US 5 (3.75 mm) DPNs or circular needle (or size needed to obtain gauge)

Stitch marker as necessary

Tapestry needle

Cable needle

SAMPLE DETAILS

Shown in Fibre Harvest Organic Merino DK (225 yd./206 m per 3.5 oz./100 g; 100% merino)

Shown in size 20 in./51 cm on model with 20.5 in./52 cm circumference head

Alternative yarn: Madelinetosh Tosh DK (225 yd./206 m per 3.5 oz./100 g; 100% merino)

GAUGE

20 sts × 28 rows to 4 in./10 cm on US 5 (3.75 mm) needles over St st

CHART

Page 130

SKILLS REQUIRED

- knit and purl stitches
- knitting in the round
- cables
- bobbles
- 3-needle bind-off or Kitchener stitch

SPECIAL STITCHES/ABBREVIATIONS

T3B = Slip next st onto cable needle and hold at back of work, knit next 2 sts, and then purl st from cable needle (right twist).

T3F = Slip next 2 sts onto cable needle and hold at front of work, purl next st, and then knit 2 sts from cable needle (left twist).

T5B = Slip next 2 sts onto cable needle and hold at back of work, knit next 3 sts, and then purl 2 sts from cable needle (right twist).

T5F = Slip next 3 sts onto cable needle and hold at front of work, purl next 2 sts, and then knit the 3 sts from cable needle (left twist).

C6B = Slip next 3 sts onto cable needle and hold at back of work, knit next 3 sts on left-hand needle, and then knit 3 sts from cable needle (right cross).

MB = Make bobble. Knit into the front and then back, then front and back, and then into the front of the next st. Turn work. Slip 1, purl 4, turn work. K2tog, k3tog, pass over st from k2tog.

INSTRUCTIONS

Using your preferred cast-on method, cast on 94 (104, 114, 124) sts, join in the round, taking care not to twist the sts. Place stitch marker to indicate start of round.

Foundation rnd: *P5, k2, p5, k6, p5, k2, p22 (27, 32, 37); rep from * to end.

BODY (Refer to Chart)

Rnd 1: *P4, T3B, p5, C6B, p5, T3F, p21 (26, 31, 36); rep from * to end.

Rnd 2: *P4, k2, p6, k6, p6, k2, p21 (26, 31, 36); rep from * to end.

Rnd 3: *P3, T3B, p4, T5B, T5F, p4, T3F, p20 (25, 30, 35); rep from * to end.

Rnd 4: *P3, k2, p5, k3, p4, k3, p5, k2, p20 (25, 30, 35); rep from * to end.

Rnd 5: *P2, T3B, p3, T5B, p4, T5F, p3, T3F, p19 (24, 29, 34); rep from * to end.

Rnd 6: *P2, k2, p1, MB, p2, k3, p8, k3, p2, MB, p1, k2, p19 (24, 29, 34); rep from * to end.

Rnd 7: *P2, T3F, p3, k3, p8, k3, p3, T3B, p19 (24, 29, 34); rep from * to end.

Rnd 8: *P3, k2, p3, k3, p8, k3, p3, k2, p20 (25, 30, 35); rep from * to end.

Rnd 9: *P3, T3F, p2, T5F, p4, T5B, p2, T3B, p20 (25, 30, 35); rep from * to end.

Rnd 10: *P4, k2, p4, k3, p4, k3, p4, k2, p21 (26, 31, 36); rep from * to end.

Rnd 11: *P4, T3F, p3, T5F, T5B, p3, T3B, p21 (26, 31, 36); rep from * to end.

Rnd 12: *P3, MB, p1, k2, p5, k6, p5, k2, p1, MB, p20 (25, 30, 35); rep from * to end.

Repeat these 12 rounds until your work measures approx. 6.75 (7.5, 8.25, 9.5) in./17 (19, 21, 24) cm, ending after an even round.

CROWN

Fold work in half so that WS are together and perform Kitchener Stitch or 3-needle bind-off to close the top.

FINISHING

Weave in all ends. A gentle wash and blocking are required to help the cables settle; avoid overstretching.

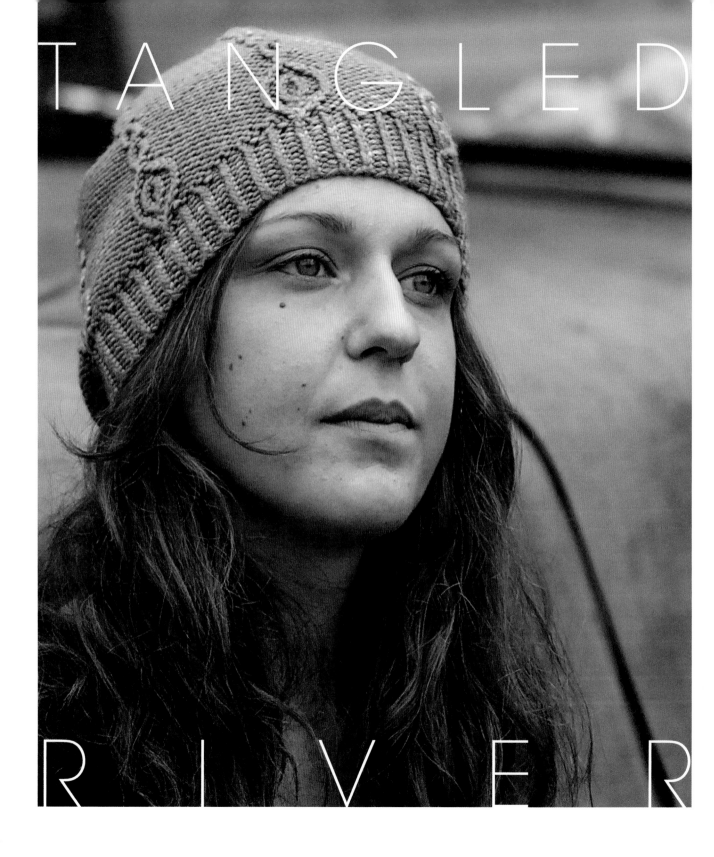

TANGLED

RIVER

SIZES

To fit sizes: 14 (17, 19, 22) in./35.5 (43.25, 48.25, 56) cm

Finished size: 12 (14.5, 16.75, 19.25) in./30.5 (36.75, 42.5, 49) cm

YARN

81 (110, 148, 188) yd./74 (101, 135, 172) m heavy DK or worsted weight (medium), plied yarn

Additional 38 yd./35 m for a 6 × 6 in./15 × 15 cm swatch in St st

NEEDLES & NOTIONS

Set each of US 5 (3.75 mm) and US 6 (4 mm) DPNs or circular needles (or sizes needed to obtain gauge)

Stitch marker as necessary

Tapestry needle

Cable needle

SAMPLE DETAILS

Shown in BabyLongLegs Semi-Precious DK (230 yd./210 m per 3.5 oz./100 g; 50% merino, 50% silk)

Shown in size 22 in./56 cm on model with 22.5 in./57.25 cm circumference head

Alternative yarn: Malabrigo Rios (210 yd./192 m per 3.5 oz./100 g; 100% superwash merino)

GAUGE

20 sts × 30 rows to 4 in./10 cm on US 6 (4 mm) needles over St st

20 sts × 30 rows to 4 in./10 cm on US 5 (3.75 mm) needles over twisted rib

CHARTS

Page 131

SKILLS REQUIRED

- knit and purl stitches
- knitting in the round
- increases and decreases
- twisted stitches
- alternating rib cable cast-on
- cables

SPECIAL STITCHES/ABBREVIATIONS

C2B = Slip next st onto cable needle and hold at back of work, knit next st through the back loop, and then knit the st from the cable needle through the back loop (right cross).

T2B = Slip next st onto cable needle and hold at back of work, knit next st through the back loop, and then purl the st from the cable needle (right twist).

T2F = Slip next st onto cable needle and hold at front of work, purl next st, and then knit next st through the back loop (left twist).

M1P = Pick up the horizontal loop between sts, place it onto the left needle, and then purl into the back of it.

I N S T R U C T I O N S

Using US 5 (3.75 mm) needles and alternating rib cable cast-on method (cast on 1 knit stitch, then 1 purl stitch, and repeat around), cast on 60 (72, 84, 96) sts.

Join in the round, being careful not to twist sts. Place stitch marker to indicate start of round.

BRIM

Now work twisted rib (k1tbl, p1) for 1 (1, 1.25, 1.5) in./2.5 (2.5, 3.25, 3.75) cm, and then work increase round once as follows:

Inc rnd: *K1tbl, p1, M1P, (k1tbl, p1) twice, (M1P, k1tbl, p1) 3 times; rep from * to end. 80 (96, 112, 128) sts

Change to US 6 needles.

BODY (Refer to Chart 1)

Note: Work all knit sts on the cables/twists through the backs of the loops.

Rnd 1: *P7, C2B, p7; rep from * to end.
Rnd 2: *P6, T2B, T2F, p6; rep from * to end.
Rnd 3: *P5, T2B, p2, T2F, p5; rep from * to end.
Rnd 4: *P4, T2B, p1, C2B, p1, T2F, p4; rep from * to end.
Rnd 5: *P4, k1tbl, p1, T2B, T2F, p1, k1tbl, p4; rep from * to end.
Rnds 6 and 7: *P4, k1tbl, p1, k1tbl, p2, k1tbl, p1, k1tbl, p4; rep from * to end.

Rnd 8: *P4, k1tbl, p1, T2F, T2B, p1, k1tbl, p4; rep from * to end.
Rnd 9: *P4, T2F, p1, C2B, p1, T2B, p4; rep from * to end.
Rnd 10: *P5, T2F, p2, T2B, p5; rep from * to end.
Rnd 11: *P6, T2F, T2B, p6; rep from * to end.
Rnds 12 and 13: *P7, C2B, p7; rep from * to end.
Rnd 14: *P6, T2B, T2F, p6; rep from * to end.
Rnds 15 and 16: *P6, k1tbl, p2, k1tbl, p6; rep from * to end.
Rnd 17: *P6, T2F, T2B, p6; rep from * to end.
Rnd 18: *P7, C2B, p7; rep from * to end.
Repeat Rnds 14–18 a further 2 (3, 4, 5) times.

CROWN (Refer to Chart 2)

Note: Continue to work all knit sts on the cables/twists through the backs of the loops.

Rnd 1: *P4, p2tog, T2B, T2F, ssp, p4; rep from * to end. 70 (84, 98, 112) sts
Rnd 2: *P3, p2tog, k1tbl, p2, k1tbl, ssp, p3; rep from * to end. 60 (72, 84, 96) sts
Rnd 3: *P4, k1tbl, p2, k1tbl, p4; rep from * to end.
Rnd 4: *P2, p2tog, T2F, T2B, ssp, p2; rep from * to end. 50 (60, 70, 80) sts
Rnd 5: *P2, p2tog, C2B, ssp, p2; rep from * to end. 40 (48, 56, 64) sts
Rnd 6: *P3, C2B, p3; rep from * to end.

Rnd 7: *P1, p2tog, C2B, ssp, p1; rep from * to end. 30 (36, 42, 48) sts

Rnd 8: *P2tog, C2B, ssp; rep from * to end. 20 (24, 28, 32) sts

Rnd 9: *K2tog, ssk; rep from * to end. 10 (12, 14, 16) sts

Rnd 10: *Ssk; rep from * to end. 5 (6, 7, 8) sts
Break yarn and draw through remaining 5 (6, 7, 8) sts; tighten to close.

FINISHING

Weave in all ends. A gentle wash and blocking are required to help the decrease lines and twisted stitches settle and lay flat.

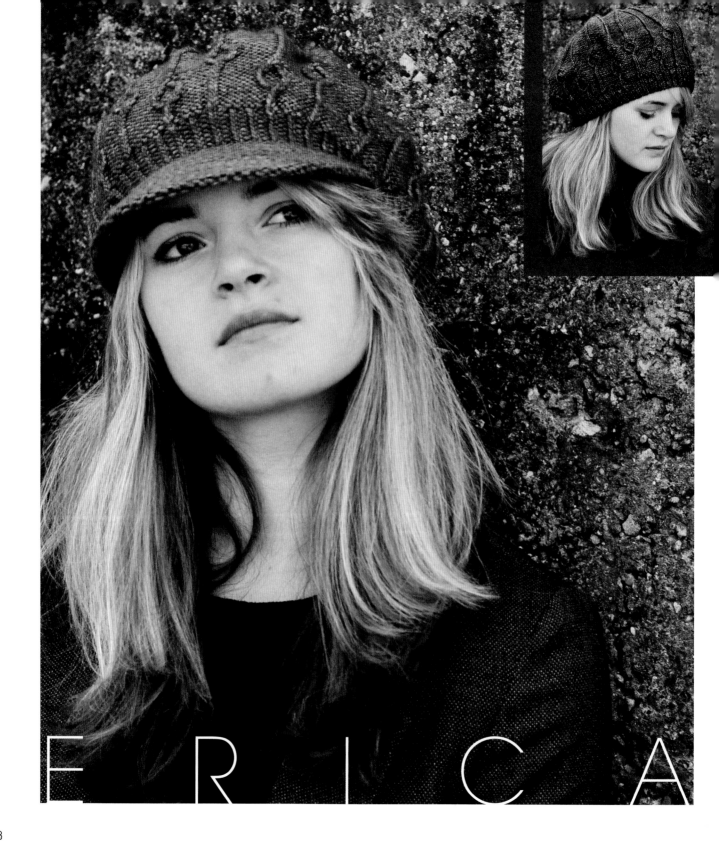

ERICA

SIZES

To fit sizes: 18 (20, 22, 24) in./45.75 (51, 56, 61) cm

Finished size: 16.25 (18.25, 20, 21.75) in./41.25 (46.25, 51, 55.25) cm

YARN

Version with Bill: 144 (184, 219.8, 261) yd./132 (169, 201, 239) m heavy DK weight (medium), multi-plied yarn

Slouchy version: 158 (196, 228, 266) yd./145 (180, 209, 244) m heavy DK weight (medium), multi-plied yarn

Additional 33 yd./31 m for a 6 × 6 in./15 × 15 cm swatch in St st

NEEDLES & NOTIONS

Set each of US 5 (3.75 mm) and US 6 (4 mm) DPNs or circular needles (or size needed to obtain gauge)

Plastic bottle or plastic canvas for Bill

Stitch marker as necessary

Tapestry needle

SAMPLE DETAILS

Shown in Fyberspates Vivacious DK (251 yd./230 m per 4.05 oz./115 g; 100% merino)

Shown in size 22 in./56 cm on model with 21.75 in./55.25 cm circumference head

GAUGE

21 sts × 30 rows to 4 in./10 cm on US 6 (4 mm) needles over St st

22 sts × 28 rows to 4 in./10 cm on US 5 (3.75 mm) needles over 1 × 1 twisted rib

CHARTS

Page 132

SKILLS REQUIRED

- knit and purl stitches
- increases and decreases
- alternating rib cable cast-on
- provisional cast-on (see page 124)
- joining live stitches
- short rows (see page 122)
- twisted stitches
- knitting in the round

SPECIAL STITCHES/ABBREVIATIONS

w&t = Wrap and turn. Bring the working yarn to the front between the needles, slip the next stitch purlwise, bring the yarn back between the needles, and slip the stitch back to the left-hand needle (stitch wrapped); turn. On the next row, work the wrap and stitch together as one.

C2B = Slip next st onto cable needle and hold at back of work, knit next st through the back loop, and then knit the st from the cable needle through the back loop (right cross).

T2B = Slip next st onto cable needle and hold at back of work, knit next st through the back loop, and then purl the st from the cable needle (right twist).

T2F = Slip next st onto cable needle and hold at front of work, purl next st, and then knit next st through the back loop (left twist).

M1P = Pick up the horizontal loop between sts, place it onto the left needle, and then purl into the back of it.

INSTRUCTIONS

VERSION WITH BILL

Using US 5 (3.75 mm) needles, waste yarn and provisional cast-on method, cast on 32 (38, 44, 50) sts. Change to main yarn.

BRIM

Row 1: Knit all sts.
Row 2: Purl all sts.

18 in./45.75 cm size: continue with Row 21
20 in./51 cm size: continue with Row 15
22 in./56 cm size: continue with Row 9
24 in./61 cm size: continue with Row 3

Row 3: K49, w&t.
Row 4: P48, w&t.
Row 5: K47, w&t.
Row 6: P46, w&t.
Row 7: K45, w&t.
Row 8: P44, w&t.
Row 9: K43, w&t.
Row 10: P42, w&t.
Row 11: K41, w&t.
Row 12: P40, w&t.
Row 13: K39, w&t.
Row 14: P38, w&t.
Row 15: K37, w&t.
Row 16: P36, w&t.
Row 17: K35, w&t.
Row 18: P34, w&t.
Row 19: K33, w&t.
Row 20: P32, w&t.
Row 21: K31, w&t.

Row 22: P30, w&t.
Row 23: K29, w&t.
Row 24: P28, w&t.
Row 25: K27, w&t.
Row 26: P26, w&t.
Row 27: K25, w&t.
Row 28: P24, w&t.
Row 29: K23, w&t.
Row 30: P22, w&t.
Row 31: K21, w&t.
Row 32: P20, w&t.
Row 33: K19, w&t.
Row 34: P18, w&t.
Row 35: K17, w&t.
Row 36: P16, w&t.
Row 37: Knit all sts, picking up the wraps as you go.
Row 38: Purl all sts, picking up the wraps as you go.

Slowly remove the provisional cast-on, stitch by stitch, and transfer all live stitches to a spare length of waste yarn. Holding both sets of stitches parallel, with the reverse St st side as the RS, lightly press the Brim with a damp cloth and iron (steam press) to create a pocket with a gentle fold; you may prefer to lightly block with pins to maintain shape.

MAKE THE PLASTIC BILL INSERT

You'll want a water bottle or similar item, ideally one in a color-coordinated plastic. Rinse the bottle and leave to dry. Cut a cross-section of the bottle deep enough for the Bill template and cut the section vertically to open it out into a rectangle. Do not attempt to remove the curve from the plastic with heat, as this will cause it to melt. Instead, cut the Bill in the direction of the curve, as this will enhance the shape when worn.

Using the schematic below, draw the curved shape onto a piece of paper and cut out. Then transfer this shape to the piece of plastic by drawing around the edge of the paper template with a permanent marker. Cut the shape out of the plastic.

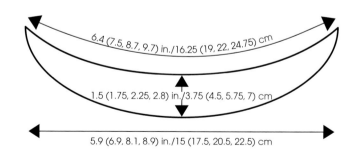

6.4 (7.5, 8.7, 9.7) in./16.25 (19, 22, 24.75) cm

1.5 (1.75, 2.25, 2.8) in./3.75 (4.5, 5.75, 7) cm

5.9 (6.9, 8.1, 8.9) in./15 (17.5, 20.5, 22.5) cm

Neaten the edges, and trim by approx. 0.1 in./2 mm all the way around. Take care not to trim too much, as you can always take more off as needed. Test the size by slipping it into the Brim pocket to see how it closes—you want a little stretch in the Brim to cover the plastic to hold it tight, but if you can see the plastic through it, the Brim has been stretched too much, and the plastic should be trimmed further.

You may also wish to make the edges smoother, particularly the points, by placing tape around the edge.

Once you have the plastic cut to shape, you will hold it inside the Brim as you close the Brim. It is easier to insert the plastic once the Brim pocket is half closed.

CLOSE BRIM POCKET

Transfer the stitches held on the length of waste yarn to a spare needle—circular needles are best for this job. Holding both sets of needles with live stitches parallel with WS together and RS (reverse St st) facing you, and keeping the plastic tucked inside the pocket throughout, work the next round as follows:

Join rnd: *Knit stitch from back needle together with the stitch from the front needle; rep from * to end. 32 (38, 44, 50) sts

BAND

Using US 5 (3.75 mm) needles, work as follows:
Using alternating rib cable cast-on method (casting on alternating knit/purl stitches), and starting with a purl stitch, cast on an additional 58 (62, 66, 70) sts (you will need to turn the work and you will cast on directly after the Brim stitches). 90 (100, 110, 120) sts

Join in the round, taking care not to twist the sts. Place stitch marker as necessary.

Next rnd: *K1tbl, p1; rep from * to end.
Repeat this round until the ribbed Band measures 0.75 (0.75, 1, 1) in./2 (2, 2.5, 2.5) cm.

Having completed the final round of the Band ribbing, slip marker, unpick 0 (2, 0, 2) sts, replace marker—this will now be the new start of the round (this action aligns the Body pattern with the Bill).

SLOUCHY VERSION

Using US 5 (3.75 mm) needles and alternating rib cable cast-on method (alternating 1 knit stitch, 1 purl stitch), cast on 90 (100, 110, 120) sts. Join in the round, taking care not to twist sts. Place stitch marker as necessary.

BAND

Next rnd: *K1tbl, p1; rep from * to end.
Repeat this round until the ribbed Band measures 1 (1, 1.25, 1.25) in./2.5 (2.5, 3.25, 3.25) cm.

BOTH VERSIONS

BODY (Refer to Chart 1)

Change to US 6 (4 mm) needles and work increase round once as follows:

Inc rnd: *(P1, M1P) twice, k1tbl, p1, M1P, p3, M1P, p1, k1tbl, M1P, p1, M1P; rep from * to end. 144 (160, 176, 192) sts

Now work Body pattern as follows, noting that all knit stitches are worked through the back of the loop.

Rnds 1, 2, and 3: *P4, k1tbl, p7, k1tbl, p3; rep from * to end.

Rnd 4: *P3, C2B, p7, k1tbl, p3; rep from * to end.

Rnd 5: *P2, T2B, T2F, p6, k1tbl, p3; rep from * to end.

Rnd 6: *P1, T2B, p2, T2F, p5, k1tbl, p3; rep from * to end.

Rnds 7 and 8: *P1, k1tbl, p4, k1tbl, p5, k1tbl, p3; rep from * to end.

Rnd 9: *P1, T2F, p2, T2B, p5, k1tbl, p3; rep from * to end.

Rnd 10: *P2, T2F, T2B, p6, k1tbl, p3; rep from * to end.

Rnd 11: *P3, T2B, p7, k1tbl, p3; rep from * to end.

Rnd 12: *P3, k1tbl, p7, C2B, p3; rep from * to end.

Rnd 13: *P3, k1tbl, p6, T2B, T2F, p2; rep from * to end.

Rnd 14: *P3, k1tbl, p5, T2B, p2, T2F, p1; rep from * to end.

Rnds 15 and 16: *P3, k1tbl, p5, k1tbl, p4, k1tbl, p1; rep from * to end.

Rnd 17: *P3, k1tbl, p5, T2F, p2, T2B, p1; rep from * to end.

Rnd 18: *P3, k1tbl, p6, T2F, T2B, p2; rep from * to end.

Rnd 19: *P3, k1tbl, p7, T2B, p3; rep from * to end.

Rnd 20: *P3, k1tbl, p7, k1tbl, p4; rep from * to end.

Repeat Rnd 20 until Body of the hat (excluding the Brim/Bill) measures:

Bill version: approx. 3 (3.5, 4, 4.5) in./7.5 (9, 10.25, 11.5) cm

Slouchy version: approx. 4 (4.5, 5, 5.5) in./10.25 (11.5, 12.75, 14) cm

CROWN SHAPING (Refer to Chart 2)

Rnd 1: *P3, k1tbl, p2tog, p5, k1tbl, p4; rep from * to end. 135 (150, 165, 180) sts

Rnd 2: *P3, k1tbl, p6, k1tbl, p4; rep from * to end.

Rnd 3: *P3, k1tbl, p4, ssp, k1tbl, p4; rep from * to end. 126 (140, 154, 168) sts

Rnd 4: *P3, k1tbl, p5, k1tbl, p4; rep from * to end.

Rnd 5: *P3, k1tbl, p2tog, p3, k1tbl, p4; rep from * to end. 117 (130, 143, 156) sts

Rnd 6: *P3, k1tbl, p2, ssp, k1tbl, p4; rep from * to end. 108 (120, 132, 144) sts

Rnd 7: *(P3, k1tbl) twice, p4; rep from * to end.

Rnd 8: *P3, k1tbl, p2tog, p1, k1tbl, p4; rep from * to end. 99 (110, 121, 132) sts

Rnd 9: *P3, k1tbl, p2, k1tbl, p4; rep from * to end.

Rnd 10: *P3, k1tbl, ssp, k1tbl, p4; rep from * to end. 90 (100, 110, 120) sts

Rnd 11: *P3, ssk, k1tbl, p4; rep from * to end. 81 (90, 99, 108) sts

Rnd 12: *P3, T2B, p4; rep from * to end.

Rnd 13: *P3, k1tbl, ssp, p3; rep from * to end. 72 (80, 88, 96) sts

Rnd 14: *P3, k1tbl, p4; rep from * to end.

Rnd 15: *P3, k1tbl, ssp, p2; rep from * to end. 63 (70, 77, 84) sts

Rnd 16: *P1, p2tog, k1tbl, p3; rep from * to end. 54 (60, 66, 72) sts

Rnd 17: *P2, k1tbl, p3; rep from * to end.

Rnd 18: *P2, k1tbl, ssp, p1; rep from * to end. 45 (50, 55, 60) sts

Rnd 19: *P2, k1tbl, p2; rep from * to end.

Rnd 20: *P2tog, k1tbl, p2; rep from * to end. 36 (40, 44, 48) sts

Rnd 21: *P1, k1tbl, ssp; rep from * to end. 27 (30, 33, 36) sts

Rnd 22: *P1, k1tbl, p1; rep from * to end.

Rnd 23: *P1, ssk; rep from * to end. 18 (20, 22, 24) sts

Rnd 24: *K2tog; rep from * to end. 9 (10, 11, 12) sts
Break yarn and draw through remaining 9 (10, 11, 12) sts; tighten to close.

FINISHING

Weave in all ends. A gentle wash and blocking are required to help the decrease lines settle and lay flat.

FOR HIM

STAGGERED

SIZES

To fit sizes: 15 (18, 20, 22, 24) in./38 (45.75, 51, 56, 61) cm

Finished size: 13.1 (15.25, 17.5, 19.7, 21.9) in./33.25 (38.75, 44.25, 50, 55.5) cm

YARN

49 (66, 85, 107, 131) yd./45 (60, 78, 98, 120) m DK weight (light), plied yarn

Additional 31 yd./28 m for a 6 × 6 in./15 × 15 cm swatch in St st

NEEDLES & NOTIONS

Set of US 3 (3.25 mm) DPNs or circular needle (or size needed to obtain gauge)

Stitch marker as necessary

Tapestry needle

SAMPLE DETAILS

Shown in Debbie Bliss Blue Faced Leicester DK (118 yd./108 m per 1.75 oz./50 g; 100% bluefaced Leicester)

Shown in size 24 in./61 cm on model with 23 in./58.5 cm circumference head (wide rib version in brown); size 22 in./56 cm on model with 21 in./53.25 cm circumference head (twisted rib version in green)

Alternative yarn: Rowan Pure Wool DK (136 yd./124 m per 3.5 oz./100 g; 100% wool)

GAUGE

22 sts × 35 rows to 4 in./10 cm on US 3 (3.25 mm) needles over St st

- knit and purl stitches
- knitting in the round
- increases and decreases
- alternating rib cable cast-on
- twisted stitches

INSTRUCTIONS

WIDE RIB VERSION
(shown in brown)

Using standard cable cast-on method, cast on 72 (84, 96, 108, 120) sts. Join in the round, being careful not to twist sts. Place stitch marker to indicate start of round.

BRIM

Rnd 1: *K3, p3; rep from * to end.
Repeat this round until brim measures 1 (1.25, 1.5, 1.75, 2) in./2.5 (3.25, 3.75, 4.5, 5) cm.

BODY

Rnd 2: *K3, p9; rep from * to end.
Repeat this round for a further 1 (1.25, 1.5, 1.75, 2) in./2.5 (3.25, 3.75, 4.5, 5) cm until work measures 2 (2.5, 3, 3.5, 4) in./5 (6.25, 7.5, 9, 10.25) cm from cast-on edge. Then work as follows:
Rnd 3: Purl all sts.
Repeat this round, forming reverse stockinette stitch, for a further 1.5 in./3.75 cm until work measures 3.5 (4, 4.5, 5, 5.5) in./9 (10.25, 11.5, 12.75, 14) cm from cast-on edge.

CROWN PREPARATION

18 in./45.75 cm size only: *P2tog, p19; rep from * to end. (80 sts)
22 in./56 cm size only: *P12, p2tog, p13; rep from * to end. (104 sts)

CROWN

15 in./38 cm size continue with Rnd 13.
18 in./45.75 cm size continue with Rnd 11.
20 in./51 cm size continue with Rnd 7.
22 in./56 cm size continue with Rnd 5.
24 in./61 cm size start at Rnd 1.

Rnd 1: *Ssp, p26, p2tog; rep from * to end. (112 sts)
Rnd 2 and all even rounds: Purl all sts.
Rnd 3: P12, p2tog, (ssp, p24, p2tog) 3 times, ssp, p12. (104 sts)
Rnd 5: *Ssp, p22, p2tog; rep from * to end. (96 sts)
Rnd 7: P10, p2tog, (ssp, p20, p2tog) 3 times, ssp, p10. (88 sts)
Rnd 9: *Ssp, p18, p2tog; rep from * to end. (80 sts)
Rnd 11: P8, p2tog, (ssp, p16, p2tog) 3 times, ssp, p8. (72 sts)
Rnd 13: *Ssp, p14, p2tog; rep from * to end. (64 sts)

Rnd 15: P6, p2tog, (ssp, p12, p2tog) 3 times, ssp, p6. (56 sts)

Rnd 17: *Ssp, p10, p2tog; rep from * to end. (48 sts)

Rnd 19: P4, p2tog, (ssp, p8, p2tog) 3 times, ssp, p4. (40 sts)

Rnd 21: *Ssp, p6, p2tog; rep from * to end. (32 sts)

Rnd 23: P2, p2tog, (ssp, p4, p2tog) 3 times, ssp, p2. (24 sts)

Rnd 25: *Ssp, p2, p2tog; rep from * to end. (16 sts)

Rnd 27: *P2tog, ssp; rep from * to end. (8 sts)

Break yarn and draw through remaining 8 sts; tighten to close.

FINISHING

Weave in all ends. A gentle wash and blocking are required to help the decreases settle and lay flat.

TWISTED RIB VERSION (shown in green)

Using alternating rib cable cast-on method (cast on alternating 1 knit stitch and 1 purl stitch), cast on 72 (84, 96, 108, 120) sts. Join in the round, being careful not to twist sts. Place stitch marker to indicate start of round.

BRIM

Rnd 1: *K1tbl, p1; rep from * to end.

Repeat this round until brim measures 1 (1.25, 1.5, 1.75, 2) in./2.5 (3.25, 3.75, 4.5, 5) cm.

BODY

Rnd 2: *K1tbl, p3; rep from * to end.

Repeat this round for a further 1 (1.25, 1.5, 1.75, 2) in./2.5 (3.25, 3.75, 4.5, 5) cm until work measures 2 (2.5, 3, 3.5, 4) in./5 (6.25, 7.5, 9, 10.25) cm from cast-on edge. Then work as follows:

Rnd 3: Purl all sts.

Repeat this round, forming reverse stockinette stitch, for a further 1.5 in./3.75 cm until work measures 3.5 (4, 4.5, 5, 5.5) in./9 (10.25, 11.5, 12.75, 14) cm from cast-on edge.

CROWN PREPARATION

18 in./45.75 cm size only: *P2tog, p19; rep from * to end. (80 sts)

22 in./56 cm size only: *P12, p2tog, p13; rep from * to end. (104 sts)

CROWN

15 in./38 cm size continue with Rnd 13.

18 in./45.75 cm size continue with Rnd 11.

20 in./51 cm size continue with Rnd 7.

22 in./56 cm size continue with Rnd 5.

24 in./61 cm size start at Rnd 1.

Rnd 1: *Ssp, p26, p2tog; rep from * to end. (112 sts)
Rnd 2 and all even rounds: Purl all sts.
Rnd 3: P12, p2tog, (ssp, p24, p2tog) 3 times, ssp, p12. (104 sts)
Rnd 5: *Ssp, p22, p2tog; rep from * to end. (96 sts)
Rnd 7: P10, p2tog, (ssp, p20, p2tog) 3 times, ssp, p10. (88 sts)
Rnd 9: *Ssp, p18, p2tog; rep from * to end. (80 sts)
Rnd 11: P8, p2tog, (ssp, p16, p2tog) 3 times, ssp, p8. (72 sts)
Rnd 13: *Ssp, p14, p2tog; rep from * to end. (64 sts)
Rnd 15: P6, p2tog, (ssp, p12, p2tog) 3 times, ssp, p6. (56 sts)

Rnd 17: *Ssp, p10, p2tog; rep from * to end. (48 sts)
Rnd 19: P4, p2tog, (ssp, p8, p2tog) 3 times, ssp, p4. (40 sts)
Rnd 21: *Ssp, p6, p2tog; rep from * to end. (32 sts)
Rnd 23: P2, p2tog, (ssp, p4, p2tog) 3 times, ssp, p2. (24 sts)
Rnd 25: *Ssp, p2, p2tog; rep from * to end. (16 sts)
Rnd 27: *P2tog, ssp; rep from * to end. (8 sts)
Break yarn and draw through remaining 8 sts; tighten to close.

FINISHING

Weave in all ends. A gentle wash and blocking are required to help the decreases settle and lay flat.

NORTHEND

<u>SIZES</u>

To fit sizes: 16 (18, 20, 22, 24) in./40.75 (45.75, 51, 56, 61) cm

Finished size: 14.25 (16, 17.7, 19.5, 21.25) in./36.25 (40.75, 45, 49.5, 54) cm

<u>YARN</u>

65 (83, 104, 128, 153) yd./59 (77, 96, 117, 140) m Aran weight (medium), plied yarn

Additional 31 yd./28 m for a 6 × 6 in./15 × 15 cm swatch in St st

<u>NEEDLES & NOTIONS</u>

Set of US 7 (4.5 mm) DPNs or circular (or size needed to obtain gauge)

Stitch marker as necessary

Tapestry needle

<u>SAMPLE DETAILS</u>

Shown in Fyberspates Scrumptious Aran (180 yd./165 m per 3.5 oz./100 g; 55% merino, 45% silk)

Shown in size 22 in./56 cm on model with 23 in./58.5 cm circumference head

<u>GAUGE</u>

18 sts × 24 rows to 4 in./10 cm on US 7 (4.5 mm) needles over St st

18 sts × 34 rows to 4 in./10 cm on US 7 (4.5 mm) needles over garter St

SKILLS REQUIRED

- knit and purl stitches
- knitting in the round
- increases and decreases
- twisted stitches
- alternating rib cable cast-on

SPECIAL STITCHES/ABBREVIATIONS

CDD = Centered double decrease. Slip two together knitwise, knit one, pass slipped sts over.

INSTRUCTIONS

Using alternating rib cable cast-on method (cast on alternating 1 knit st with 1 purl st), cast on 64 (72, 80, 88, 96) sts.

Join in the round, being careful not to twist stitches. Place stitch marker to indicate start of round.

BRIM

Now work twisted rib (k1tbl, p1) until work measures 1.75 (2, 2.25, 2.5, 2.75) in./4.5 (5, 5.75, 6.5, 7) cm from cast-on edge.

BODY

Rnd 1: *Sl 1, p15 (17, 19, 21, 23); rep from * to end.
Rnd 2: *K1tbl, k15 (17, 19, 21, 23); rep from * to end.
These two rounds form the Body pattern. Repeat these two rounds until work measures 3.5 (4, 4.5, 5, 5.5) in./9 (10.25, 11.5, 12.75, 14) cm from the cast-on edge, 1.75 (2, 2.25, 2.5, 2.75) in./4.5 (5, 5.75, 6.5, 7) cm from start of Body section, ending after a Rnd 1.

CROWN

16 in./40.75 cm size continue with Rnd 9
18 in./45.75 cm size continue with Rnd 7
20 in./51 cm size continue with Rnd 5
22 in./56 cm size continue with Rnd 3
24 in./61 cm size start at Rnd 1

Rnd 1: *K1tbl, k2tog, k19, ssk; rep from * to end. (88 sts)
Rnd 2: *Sl 1, p21; rep from * to end.
Rnd 3: *K1tbl, k2tog, k17, ssk; rep from * to end. (80 sts)
Rnd 4: *Sl 1, p19; rep from * to end.
Rnd 5: *K1tbl, k2tog, k15, ssk; rep from * to end. (72 sts)
Rnd 6: *Sl 1, p17; rep from * to end.
Rnd 7: *K1tbl, k2tog, k13, ssk; rep from * to end. (64 sts)
Rnd 8: *Sl 1, p15; rep from * to end.
Rnd 9: *K1tbl, k2tog, k11, ssk; rep from * to end. (56 sts)
Rnd 10: *Sl 1, p13; rep from * to end.
Rnd 11: *K1tbl, k2tog, k9, ssk; rep from * to end. (48 sts)
Rnd 12: *Sl 1, p11; rep from * to end.
Rnd 13: *K1tbl, k2tog, k7, ssk; rep from * to end. (40 sts)
Rnd 14: *Sl 1, p9; rep from * to end.
Rnd 15: *K1tbl, k2tog, k5, ssk; rep from * to end. (32 sts)
Rnd 16: *Sl 1, p7; rep from * to end.
Rnd 17: *K1tbl, k2tog, k3, ssk; rep from * to end. (24 sts)
Rnd 18: *Sl 1, p5; rep from * to end.
Rnd 19: *K1tbl, k2tog, k1, ssk; rep from * to end. (16 sts)
Rnd 20: *Sl 1, p3; rep from * to end.
Rnd 21: *K1tbl, CDD; rep from * to end. (8 sts)
Break yarn and draw through remaining 8 sts; tighten to close.

FINISHING

Weave in all ends. A gentle wash and blocking are required to help the decrease lines settle and lay flat.

CHEVRON

SIZES

To fit sizes: 20 (22, 24) in./51 (56, 61) cm

Finished size: 18 (20.5, 22.5) in./45.75 (52, 57.25) cm

YARN

87 (109, 130) yd./82 (100, 119) m Aran weight (medium), plied yarn

Additional 26 yd./25 m for a 6 × 6 in./15 × 15 cm swatch in St st

NEEDLES & NOTIONS

Set of US 7 (4.5 mm) DPNs or circular (or size needed to obtain gauge)

Stitch marker as necessary

Tapestry needle

Cable needle

SAMPLE DETAILS

Shown in Jamieson & Smith Shetland Aran (98.5 yd./90 m per 1.75 oz./50 g; 100% wool)

Shown in size 24 in./61 cm on model with 23 in./58.5 cm circumference head

Alternative yarn: Ístex Létt-Lopi (109 yd./100 m per 1.75 oz./ 50 g; 100% Icelandic wool)

GAUGE

17 sts × 25 rows to 4 in./10 cm on US 7 (4.5 mm) needles over St st

25.5 sts × 27 rows to 4 in./10 cm on US 7 (4.5 mm) needles over cable stitch pattern

SKILLS REQUIRED

- knit and purl stitches
- knitting in the round
- increases and decreases
- cable cast-on
- cables

SPECIAL STITCHES/ABBREVIATIONS

T3F = Slip next 2 sts onto cable needle and hold at front of work, purl next st, and then knit 2 sts from cable needle (left twist).

T3B = Slip next st onto cable needle and hold at back of work, knit next 2 sts, and then purl st from cable needle (right twist).

INSTRUCTIONS

Using cable cast-on method, cast on 96 (108, 120) sts. Join in the round, being careful not to twist sts. Place stitch marker to indicate start of round.

BRIM (Refer to Chart)

Rnd 1: *K2, p4; rep from * to end.
Rnd 2: *T3F, p3; rep from * to end.
Rnd 3: *P1, T3F, p2; rep from * to end.
Rnd 4: *P2, T3F, p1; rep from * to end.
Rnds 5 to 12: *P3, T3F; rep from * to end, RM, p1, PM.
Rnd 13: *P3, T3F; rep from * to end, do not move marker.
Rnd 14: *P4, k2; rep from * to end.
Rnd 15: *P3, T3B; rep from * to end.

Rnd 16: *P2, T3B, p1; rep from * to end.
Rnd 17: *P1, T3B, p2; rep from * to end.
Rnds 18 to 25: *T3B, p3; rep from * to last 6 sts, T3B, p2, slip last purl st just made back to left-hand needle and PM for new beg of round. (Purl st becomes 1st st of Rnd 26.)
Rnd 26: *T3B, p3; rep from * to end, do not move marker.
Rnd 27: *K2tog, p1, p2tog, p1; rep from * to end. 64 (72, 80) sts

BODY

Work 0 (3, 6) rounds of reverse stockinette stitch (purl every stitch).

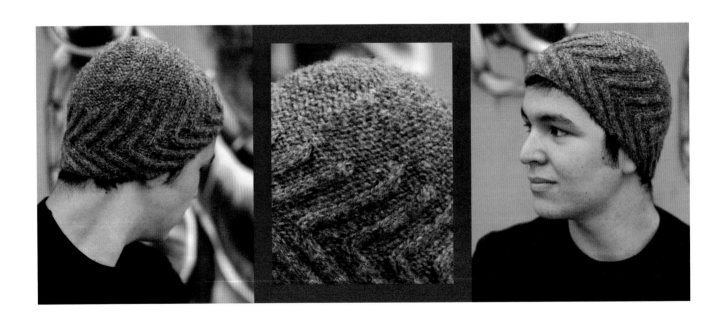

CROWN

20 in./51 cm size continue with Rnd 5.
22 in./56 cm size continue with Rnd 3.
24 in./61 cm size start at Rnd 1.

Rnd 1: *P18, p2tog; rep from * to end. (76 sts)
Rnd 2: *P17, p2tog; rep from * to end. (72 sts)
Rnd 3: *P16, p2tog; rep from * to end. (68 sts)
Rnd 4: *P15, p2tog; rep from * to end. (64 sts)
Rnd 5: *P14, p2tog; rep from * to end. (60 sts)
Rnd 6: *P13, p2tog; rep from * to end. (56 sts)
Rnd 7: *P12, p2tog; rep from * to end. (52 sts)
Rnd 8: *P11, p2tog; rep from * to end. (48 sts)
Rnd 9: *P10, p2tog; rep from * to end. (44 sts)
Rnd 10: *P9, p2tog; rep from * to end. (40 sts)
Rnd 11: *P8, p2tog; rep from * to end. (36 sts)
Rnd 12: *P7, p2tog; rep from * to end. (32 sts)
Rnd 13: *P6, p2tog; rep from * to end. (28 sts)
Rnd 14: *P5, p2tog; rep from * to end. (24 sts)
Rnd 15: *P4, p2tog; rep from * to end. (20 sts)
Rnd 16: *P3, p2tog; rep from * to end. (16 sts)
Rnd 17: *P2, p2tog; rep from * to end. (12 sts)
Rnd 18: *P1, p2tog; rep from * to end. (8 sts)

Break yarn and draw through remaining 8 sts and tighten to close.

FINISHING

Weave in all ends. A gentle wash and blocking are required to help the decreases settle and lay flat.

CHART

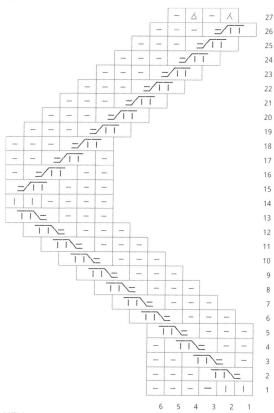

KEY

☐ = Knit.

☐ = Purl.

☐ = Knit next 2 stitches together.

☐ = Purl next 2 stitches together.

☐ = T3F. Slip next 2 sts onto cable needle and hold at front of work, purl next st, and then knit 2 sts from cable needle (left twist).

☐ = T3B. Slip next st onto cable needle and hold at back of work, knit next 2 sts, and then purl st from cable needle (right twist).

T U R B I N E

SIZES

To fit sizes: 19.5 (21, 22.5, 24) in./49.5 (53.5, 57.25, 61) cm
Finished size: 16.5 (17.9, 19.5, 21) in./42 (45.5, 49.5, 53.5) cm

YARN

83 (98.5, 115, 132) yd./76 (90, 107, 124) m Aran weight (medium), plied yarn
Additional 26 yd./25 m for a 6 × 6 in./15 × 15 cm swatch in St st

NEEDLES & NOTIONS

Set of US 7 (4.5 mm) DPNs or circular needle (or size needed to obtain gauge)
Stitch marker as necessary
Tapestry needle
Cable needle

SAMPLE DETAILS

Shown in Jamieson & Smith Shetland Aran (98.5 yd./90 m per 1.75 oz./50 g; 100% wool)
Shown in size 22.5 in./57.25 cm on model with 23 in./58.5 cm circumference head
Alternative yarn: Ístex Létt-Lopi (109 yd./100 m per 1.75 oz./50 g; 100% Icelandic wool)

GAUGE

17 sts × 25 rows to 4 in./10 cm on US 7 (4.5 mm) needles over St st

SKILLS REQUIRED

- knit and purl stitches
- knitting in the round
- increases and decreases
- cable cast-on
- cables

SPECIAL STITCHES/ABBREVIATIONS

T3F = Slip next 2 sts onto cable needle and hold at front of work, purl next st, and then knit 2 sts from cable needle (left twist).
T4FD = Slip next 2 sts onto cable needle and hold at front of work, purl next 2 sts together, and then knit 2 sts from cable needle (left twist and decrease).

I N S T R U C T I O N S

Using cable cast-on method, cast on 78 (84, 90, 96) sts. Join in the round, being careful not to twist sts. Place stitch marker to indicate start of round.

Work foundation round once as follows:

Foundation rnd: *P14 (16, 18, 20), (k2, p3) twice, k2; rep from * to end, RM, p1, PM.

BODY (Refer to Chart 1)

Rnd 1: *P13 (15, 17, 19), (T3F, p2) twice, T3F; rep from * to end, RM, p1, PM.

Repeat this round until Body of hat measures approximately 4.25 (4.75, 5.25, 5.75) in./11 (12, 13.5, 14.5) cm or desired length.

CROWN (Refer to Chart 2)

19.5 in./49.5 cm size continue with Rnd 5.
21 in./53.5 cm size continue with Rnd 4.
22.5 in./57.25 cm size continue with Rnd 2.
24 in./61 cm size start at Rnd 1.

Rnd 1: *P2tog, p15, p2tog, (T3F, p2) twice, T3F; rep from * to end, RM, p1, PM. (90 sts)

Rnd 2: *P2tog, p13, p2tog, (T3F, p2) twice, T3F; rep from * to end, RM, p1, PM. (84 sts)

Rnd 3: *P15, (T3F, p2) twice, T3F; rep from * to end, RM, p1, PM.

Rnd 4: *P2tog, p11, p2tog, (T3F, p2) twice, T3F; rep from * to end, RM, p1, PM. (78 sts)

CHART 1

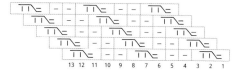

CHART 2

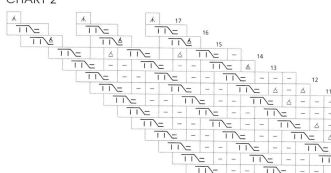

KEY

- ☐ = Knit.
- ☐ = Purl.
- ◹ = Purl next 2 sts together.
- ◹ = Purl next 3 sts together.
- ⋏ = Knit next 3 sts together.
- T3F. Slip next 2 sts onto cable needle and hold at front of work, purl next st, and then knit 2 sts from cable needle (left twist).
- T4FD. Slip next 2 sts onto cable needle and hold at front of work, purl next 2 sts together, and then knit 2 sts from cable needle (left twist and decrease).

Rnd 5: *P2tog, p9, p2tog, (T3F, p2) twice, T3F; rep from * to end, RM, p1, PM. (72 sts)

Rnd 6: *P11, (T3F, p2) twice, T3F; rep from * to end, RM, p1, PM.

Rnd 7: *P2tog, p7, p2tog, (T3F, p2) twice, T3F; rep from * to end, RM, p1, PM. (66 sts)

Rnd 8: *P2tog, p5, p2tog, (T3F, p2) twice, T3F; rep from * to end, RM, p1, PM. (60 sts)

Rnd 9: *P7, (T3F, p2) twice, T3F; rep from * to end, RM, p1, PM.

Rnd 10: *P2tog, p3, p2tog, (T3F, p2) twice, T3F; rep from * to end, RM, p1, PM. (54 sts)

Rnd 11: *P2tog, p1, p2tog, (T3F, p2) twice, T3F; rep from * to end, RM, p1, PM. (48 sts)

Rnd 12: *P3, (T3F, p2) twice, T3F; rep from * to end, RM, p1, PM.

Rnd 13: *P3tog, (T3F, p2) twice, T3F; rep from * to end, RM, p1, PM. (42 sts)

Rnd 14: *P1, (T3F, p2tog) twice, T3F; rep from * to end, RM, p2, PM. (36 sts)

Rnd 15: *T4FD; rep from * to end, RM, p1, PM. (27 sts)

Rnd 16: *T3F; rep from * to end.

Rnd 17: *K3tog; rep from * to end. (9 sts)

Break yarn and draw through remaining 9 sts; tighten to close.

FINISHING

Weave in all ends. A gentle wash and blocking are required to help the decreases settle and lay flat.

LEDGER

BEANIE

SIZES

To fit sizes: 16 (18, 20, 22, 24) in./40.75 (45.75, 51, 56, 61) cm

Finished size: 14.5 (16, 17.5, 19.25, 20.75) in./36.75 (40.75, 44.5, 49, 52.75) cm

YARN

61 (76.5, 94, 114, 135) yd./55 (70, 86, 104, 124) m heavy DK or worsted weight (medium), plied yarn

Additional 32 yd./29 m for a 6 × 6 in./15 × 15 cm swatch in St st

NEEDLES & NOTIONS

Set of US 6 (4 mm) DPNs or circular needle (or size needed to obtain gauge)

Stitch marker as necessary

Tapestry needle

SAMPLE DETAILS

Shown in KnitPicks Gloss DK (main photo) (122.5 yd./112 m per 1.75 oz./50 g; 70% merino, 30% silk)

Shown in size 24 in./61 cm on model with 23 in./58.5 cm circumference head

Also shown in Cascade 220 Venezia Worsted (218 yd./199 m per 3.5 oz./100 g; 70% merino, 30% silk)

Shown in size 20 in./51 cm on model with 19.5 in./49.5 cm circumference head

GAUGE

20 sts × 26 rows to 4 in./10 cm on US 6 (4 mm) needles over St st

20 sts × 26 rows to 4 in./10 cm on US 6 (4 mm) needles over ribbing, relaxed

SKILLS REQUIRED

- knit and purl stitches
- knitting in the round
- increases and decreases
- alternating 2 × 2 rib cable cast-on

INSTRUCTIONS

Using alternating cable cast-on method for 2 × 2 ribbing, cast on 72 (80, 88, 96, 104) sts.

Join in the round, being careful not to twist sts. Place stitch marker to indicate start of round.

BRIM

Now work k2, p2 rib for 1.5 (1.75, 2, 2.25, 2.5) in./3.75 (4.5, 5, 5.75, 6.25) cm (or desired length), and then proceed to Body.

BODY

Now work k1, p1 rib for 2 (2.25, 2.5, 2.75, 3) in./5 (5.75, 6.25, 7, 7.5) cm (or desired length), and then proceed to Crown.

CROWN

16 in./40.75 cm size continue with Rnd 9.
18 in./45.75 cm size continue with Rnd 7.
20 in./51 cm size continue with Rnd 5.
22 in./56 cm size continue with Rnd 3.
24 in./61 cm size start at Rnd 1.

Rnd 1: *(K1, p1) 11 times, k1, k2tog, p1; rep from * to end. (100 sts)

Rnd 2: *(K1, p1) 11 times, k2tog, p1; rep from * to end. (96 sts)

Rnd 3: *(K1, p1) 10 times, k1, k2tog, p1; rep from * to end. (92 sts)

Rnd 4: *(K1, p1) 10 times, k2tog, p1; rep from * to end. (88 sts)

Rnd 5: *(K1, p1) 9 times, k1, k2tog, p1; rep from * to end. (84 sts)

Rnd 6: *(K1, p1) 9 times, k2tog, p1; rep from * to end. (80 sts)

Rnd 7: *(K1, p1) 8 times, k1, k2tog, p1; rep from * to end. (76 sts)

Rnd 8: *(K1, p1) 8 times, k2tog, p1; rep from * to end. (72 sts)

Rnd 9: *(K1, p1) 7 times, k1, k2tog, p1; rep from * to end. (68 sts)

Rnd 10: *(K1, p1) 7 times, k2tog, p1; rep from * to end. (64 sts)

Rnd 11: *(K1, p1) 6 times, k1, k2tog, p1; rep from * to end. (60 sts)

Rnd 12: *(K1, p1) 6 times, k2tog, p1; rep from * to end. (56 sts)

Rnd 13: *(K1, p1) 5 times, k1, k2tog, p1; rep from * to end. (52 sts)

Rnd 14: *(K1, p1) 5 times, k2tog, p1; rep from * to end. (48 sts)

Rnd 15: *(K1, p1) 4 times, k1, k2tog, p1; rep from * to end. (44 sts)

Rnd 16: *(K1, p1) 4 times, k2tog, p1; rep from * to end. (40 sts)

Rnd 17: *(K1, p1) 3 times, k1, k2tog, p1; rep from * to end. (36 sts)

Rnd 18: *(K1, p1) 3 times, k2tog, p1; rep from * to end. (32 sts)

Rnd 19: *(K1, p1) twice, k1, k2tog, p1; rep from * to end. (28 sts)

Rnd 20: *(K1, p1) twice, k2tog, p1; rep from * to end. (24 sts)

Rnd 21: *K1, p1, k1, k2tog, p1; rep from * to end. (20 sts)

Rnd 22: *K1, p1, k2tog, p1; rep from * to end. (16 sts)

Rnd 23: *K1, k2tog, p1; rep from * to end. (12 sts)
Break yarn and draw through remaining 12 sts; tighten to close.

FINISHING

Weave in all ends. A gentle wash and blocking are required to help the decrease lines settle and lay flat.

FOR KIDS

INCATENATO

SIZES

To fit size: 16 (18, 20, 22) in./40.75 (45.75, 51, 56) cm

Finished size: 13 (15.25, 17.5, 19.75) in./33 (38.75, 44.5, 50.25) cm

YARN

Yarn A: 42 (58, 76.5, 97) yd./38 (53, 70, 89) m heavy DK or light worsted weight (medium), plied yarn

Yarn B: 52 (72, 94, 121) yd./47 (65, 86, 110) m heavy DK or light worsted weight (medium), plied yarn

Additional 46 yd./42 m for a 6 × 6 in./15 × 15 cm swatch in garter st

NEEDLES & NOTIONS

Set of US 4 (3.5 mm) DPNs or circular needle (or size needed to obtain gauge)

US 7 (4.5 mm) single need for binding off

Stitch marker as necessary

US E-4 (3.5 mm) crochet hook

Approx. 1 yd./1 m waste yarn

Tapestry needle

SAMPLE DETAILS

Shown in Meadowyarn Fell Worsted (252 yd./230 m per 4.05 oz./115 g; 100% superwash merino)

Shown in size 20 in./51 cm on model with 21.5 in./54.5 cm circumference head

GAUGE

22 sts × 44 rows to 4 in./10 cm on US 4 (3.5 mm) needles over garter st

CHART

Page 133

SKILLS REQUIRED

- knit and purl stitches
- knitting in the round
- increases and decreases
- slipped stitches
- provisional cast-on (see page 124)
- grafting (see page 120)

HINT

Slip stitches purlwise. The yarn will lie behind the work.

SPECIAL STITCHES/ABBREVIATIONS

kbf = Knit into the back and front of next st.

(A) = Work with Yarn A.

(B) = Work with Yarn B.

INSTRUCTIONS

Using waste yarn and crochet provisional cast-on method, cast on 10 (13, 16, 19) sts. Change to Yarn A and with smaller needles work the Brim as follows:

BRIM

Row 1 (WS): Knit to last stitch, bring yarn forward, slip stitch purlwise, turn (creating a slipped-stitch selvedge).
Row 2 (RS): Knit all sts.
Repeat Rows 1 and 2, continuing to work a slipped-stitch selvedge on one side only throughout the Brim, until 36 (42, 48, 54) rows/18 (21, 24, 27) ridges have been worked, where 1 ridge = 2 rows.

Note: When you are counting ridges, ensure that the ridge count on both sides of the work is the same, remembering to include the ridge created with the provisional cast-on. This method ensures that an even number of rows have been worked.

Row 3 (WS): K1, k2tog, knit to last stitch, bring yarn forward, slip stitch purlwise, turn.
Row 4 (RS): Knit all sts.
Repeat Rows 3 and 4 a total of 4 (5, 6, 7) times until 6 (8, 10, 12) sts remain, and then repeat Rows 1 and 2 for a further 56 (64, 72, 80) rows/28 (32, 36, 40) ridges.

Row 5 (WS): K1, kbf, knit to last stitch, bring yarn forward, slip stitch purlwise, and turn.
Row 6 (RS): Knit all sts.
Repeat Rows 5 and 6 a total of 4 (5, 6, 7) times until you have 10 (13, 16, 19) sts, and then repeat Rows 1 and 2 for a further 34 (40, 46, 52) rows/17 (20, 23, 26) ridges.

Note: A total of 142 (166, 190, 214) rows/71 (83, 95, 107) ridges have been worked up to this point.

Then work Row 1 once more, leaving the yarn at the back of the work. Break yarn.

Carefully remove provisional cast-on stitch by stitch, taking care to keep in pattern, transferring live stitches to second needle. Prepare your stitches per the tutorial on page 120, and you will be performing garter stitch grafting across all sts. However, as you will begin grafting from the slipped-stitch edge, to maintain the edge pattern, work the selvedge and first stitch as follows:

SELVEDGE EDGE

Front needle: Insert needle purlwise, leave stitch on needle.
Back needle: Insert needle knitwise, leave stitch on needle.

FIRST STITCH

Front needle: Insert needle knitwise, slip stitch off needle; insert needle purlwise into next stitch, leave stitch on needle.
Back needle: Insert needle purlwise, slip stitch off needle; insert needle purlwise into next stitch, leave stitch on needle.
Then continue all subsequent stitches per the Kitchener stitch for garter stitch tutorial (see page 120). (Essentially, this maneuver works a stockinette stitch graft selvedge, and the first half of each stitch on the back and front needles as stockinette stitch too. You may find that you need to adjust these to get a perfect slipped-stitch edge, depending on how your stitches have been released, but this will be sufficient to maintain the pattern.) Weave in all ends. You may wish to use the yarn tail to neaten the selvedge edge. The garter graft will have created a final row in the work, bringing the total number of ridges to 72 (84, 96, 108).

BODY, PART 1 (Refer to Chart)

With smaller needles and starting at the point of grafting with the slipped-stitch edge upward and visible with the RS facing, pick up but do not knit one stitch for each garter ridge: pick up the stitch one stitch in from the edge on the WS, which would be the first ridge directly below the rear of the slipped stitch. 72 (84, 96, 108) sts

Starting with Yarn B, work mosaic pattern as follows:

Rnd 1: (B) knit all sts.
Rnd 2: (B) purl all sts.
Rnd 3: *Sl 2, (A) k9, sl 1; rep from * to end.
Rnd 4: *Sl 2, (A) p9, sl 1; rep from * to end.
Rnd 5: *(B) k2, sl 1, k7, sl 1, k1; rep from * to end.
Rnd 6: *(B) p2, sl 1, p7, sl 1, p1; rep from * to end.
Rnd 7: *Sl 2, (A) k1, sl 1, k5, sl 1, k1, sl 1; rep from * to end.
Rnd 8: *Sl 2, (A) p1, sl 1, p5, sl 1, p1, sl 1; rep from * to end.

Rnd 9: *(B) k2, sl 1, k1, sl 1, k3, sl 1, k1, sl 1, k1; rep from * to end.
Rnd 10: *(B) p2, sl 1, p1, sl 1, p3, sl 1, p1, sl 1, p1; rep from * to end.
Rnd 11: *(A) k6, sl 1, k5; rep from * to end.
Rnd 12: *(A) p6, sl 1, p5; rep from * to end.
Rnd 13: *(B) k5, sl 1, k1, sl 1, k4; rep from * to end.
Rnd 14: *(B) p5, sl 1, p1, sl 1, p4; rep from * to end.
Rnds 15 and 16: Work as Rnds 11 and 12.
Rnds 17 and 18: Work as Rnds 9 and 10.
Rnds 19 and 20: Work as Rnds 7 and 8.
Rnds 21 and 22: Work as Rnds 5 and 6.
Rnds 23 and 24: Work as Rnds 3 and 4.
Rnds 25 and 26: Work as Rnds 1 and 2.
Rnd 27: (B) knit all sts.

Using larger needle and Yarn A, bind off stitches loosely.

BODY, PART 2

With RS facing, using a smaller needle, and starting at the center back/grafting point, pick up but do not knit 72 (84, 96, 108) sts on the reverse of the bind-off.

Slip 18 (21, 24, 27) sts. This point, the side of the hat, will now be the new round starting point.

You will continue this section in Yarn B only.

Rnd 1: *K1tbl, k35 (41, 47, 53); rep from * to end.

Rnd 2: *Sl 1, p35 (41, 47, 53); rep from * to end.

Repeat these two rounds until a total of 10 (13, 16, 19) ridges have been worked, ending after Rnd 2.

CROWN

With Yarn A, sl 1, k35 (41, 47, 53).

Fold work in half so that WS are together. Break Yarn A, leaving a 1 yd./1 m tail.

Thread the yarn through the first slipped stitch and slip it off the needle; perform Kitchener stitch for garter stitch across all sts until the final slipped stitch remains; thread the yarn through the slipped stitch to finish.

FINISHING

Weave in all ends. A gentle wash and blocking are required to help the decrease lines settle and lay flat.

TORSIONE

SIZES

To fit size: 14 (16, 18, 20, 22) in./35.5 (40.75, 45.75, 51, 56) cm

Finished size: 13.25 (14.75, 16, 17.25, 18.75) in./33.75 (37.5, 40.75, 43.75, 47.75) cm

YARN

Yarn A: 54 (67, 83, 102, 122.5) yd./50 (61, 76, 93, 112) m DK weight (light), plied yarn

Yarn B: 72 (92, 110, 130, 151) yd./65 (84, 101, 119, 139) m DK weight (light), plied yarn

Additional 47 yd./43 m for a 6 × 6 in./15 × 15 cm swatch in St st

NEEDLES & NOTIONS

Set of US 5 (3.75 mm) DPNs or circular needle (or size needed to obtain gauge)

US F-5 (3.75 mm) crochet hook

Spare needles to aid with crown construction

Stitch marker as necessary

Tapestry needle

SAMPLE DETAILS

Shown in Fyberspates Vivacious DK (251 yd./230 m per 3.5 oz./100 g; 100% merino)

Shown in size 20 in./51 cm on model with 21 in./53.25 cm circumference head

GAUGE

23 sts × 35 rows to 4 in./10 cm on US 5 (3.75 mm) needles over St st

24 sts × 36 rows to 4 in./10 cm on US 5 (3.75 mm) needles over twisted rib

SKILLS REQUIRED

- knit and purl stitches
- knitting in the round
- increases and decreases
- alternating rib cable cast-on
- crochet bind-off
- stranded knitting techniques

SPECIAL STITCHES/ABBREVIATIONS

(A) = Work with Yarn A.

(B) = Work with Yarn B.

INSTRUCTIONS

Using Yarn A and alternating rib cable cast-on method (cast on alternating knit 1 stitch, purl 1 stitch), cast on 80 (88, 96, 104, 112) sts.

Join in the round, being careful not to twist sts. Place stitch marker to indicate start of round.

BRIM

Now work (k1tbl, p1) rib for 1 (1, 1.25, 1.5, 1.75) in./2.5 (2.5, 3.25, 3.75, 4.5) cm (or desired length).

BODY

Now work foundation round once as follows before continuing in the Body pattern:

Foundation rnd: *With Yarn A k1, with Yarn B k3, M1R; rep from * to end. 100 (110, 120, 130, 140) sts

Rnd 1: *(A) k1, (B) k2tog, k2, M1R; rep from * to end.

Repeat this round until work measures 5.25 (6, 6.75, 7.5, 8.25) in./13.5 (15.25, 17.25, 19, 21) cm from cast-on edge.

Next rnd: With Yarn A, knit all sts.

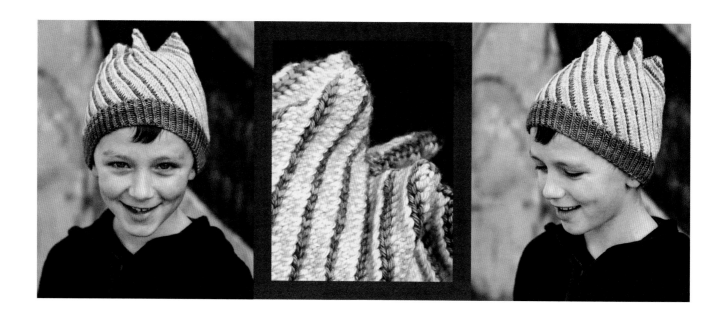

CROWN

The stitches will now be divided to close for the top.

With WS together and with RS facing, now slip the first 10 (11, 12, 13, 14) sts from the left needle directly after marker onto the first spare needle, and then slip the next 10 (11, 12, 13, 14) sts onto a second spare needle.

Bring both needles together, with WS together and with RS and first needle at the back, and starting from the right, work crochet bind-off across all sts. Where one needle has one stitch more, start the bind-off from this needle first. When the bind-off is finished, slip remaining stitch from hook back to first spare needle, where it will be included in the next peak bind-off.

Slip 11 (12, 13, 14, 15) sts onto first spare needle, and the following 10 (11, 12, 13, 14) sts onto second spare needle. Repeat the bind-off process as per the first peak—you will be working from the tip of the point inward. Repeat the process for the second peak again to form the third and fourth peaks.

You should have 21 (23, 25, 27, 29) sts remaining (including the stitch left over from the previous peak). Divide these evenly across two needles and repeat the bind-off process again to form the fifth peak.

Using either scrap yarn or a nearby yarn tail, thread through remaining stitch left from bind-off and fasten on the WS. Use remainder of yarn to close the hole at the center.

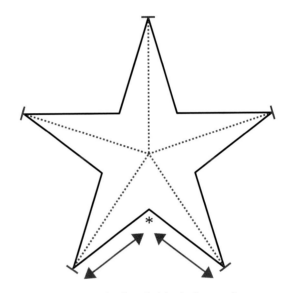

✱ = center back (start of round)

FINISHING

Weave in all ends. A gentle wash and blocking are required to help the shaping settle.

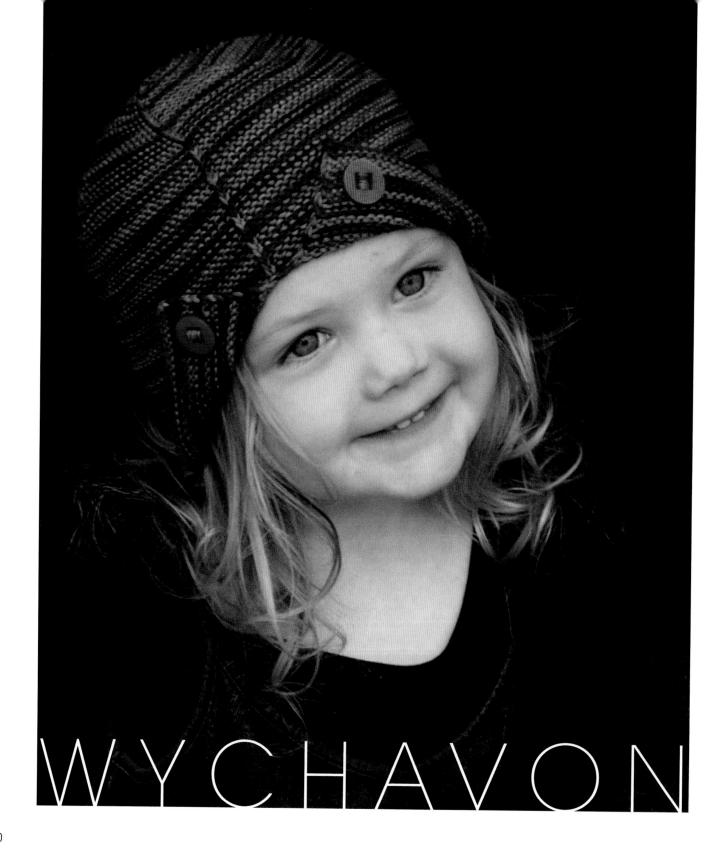

WYCHAVON

SIZES

To fit size: 15 (17, 19, 21, 23) in./38 (43.25, 48.25, 53.25, 58.5) cm

Finished size: 13.75 (15.5, 17.25, 19, 20.75) in./35 (39.5, 43.75, 48.25, 52.75) cm

YARN

122 (157, 203, 247, 353.2) yd./111 (143, 185, 226, 323) m sock/fingering/4-ply weight (super fine) yarn

Additional 53 yd./48 m for a 6 × 6 in./15 × 15 cm swatch in garter st

NEEDLES & NOTIONS

Set US 1 (2.25 mm) DPNs or circular needle (or size needed to obtain gauge)

Stitch marker as necessary

US B-1 (2.25 mm) crochet hook

Tapestry needle

Two 0.75 in (20 mm) buttons

SAMPLE DETAILS

Shown in Wollmeise Pure (574 yd./525 m per 5.3 oz./150 g; 100% merino)

Shown in size 19 in./48.25 cm on model with 18 in./45.75 cm circumference head

GAUGE

28 sts × 42 rows to 4 in./10 cm on US 1 (2.25 mm) needles over St st

28 sts × 56 rows to 4 in./10 cm on US 1 (2.25 mm) needles over garter st

SKILLS REQUIRED

- knit and purl stitches
- knitting in the round
- increases and decreases
- provisional cast-on (see page 124)

HINT

Slip stitches purlwise. The yarn will lie behind the work.

INSTRUCTIONS

Using crochet provisional cast-on method as a permanent cast-on, cast on 97 (109, 121, 133, 145) sts.

BRIM

Row 1: Knit to last stitch, bring yarn forward, slip stitch purlwise, turn (creates a slipped-stitch selvedge).
Repeat this row, continuing to work a slipped-stitch selvedge on both edges, until work measures 1.5 (1.7, 2, 2.5, 3) in./3.75 (4.25, 5, 6.25, 7.5) cm.
Prepare to join in the round, being careful not to twist sts, and then work preparation round once as follows:
Preparation rnd: Purl to last stitch, knit this stitch together through the backs of the loops with the first stitch of the next round. Place stitch marker to indicate the start of the round. 96 (108, 120, 132, 144) sts

BODY

Rnd 1: Knit all sts.
Rnd 2: Purl to last stitch, sl 1.
Repeat these two rounds until work measures 5 (5.75, 6.5, 7.5, 8.5) in./12.75 (14.5, 16.5, 19, 21.5) cm from cast-on edge, ending after a Rnd 2.

CROWN

15 in./38 cm size continue with Rnd 17.
17 in./43.25 cm size continue with Rnd 13.
19 in./48.25 cm size continue with Rnd 9.
21 in./53.25 cm size continue with Rnd 5.
23 in./58.5 cm size start at Rnd 1.

Rnd 1: *K2tog, k22; rep from * to end. (138 sts)
Rnd 2 and all even-numbered rounds: Purl to last stitch, sl 1.
Rnd 3: *K2tog, k21; rep from * to end. (132 sts)
Rnd 5: *K2tog, k20; rep from * to end. (126 sts)
Rnd 7: *K2tog, k19; rep from * to end. (120 sts)
Rnd 9: *K2tog, k18; rep from * to end. (114 sts)
Rnd 11: *K2tog, k17; rep from * to end. (108 sts)
Rnd 13: *K2tog, k16; rep from * to end. (102 sts)
Rnd 15: *K2tog, k15; rep from * to end. (96 sts)
Rnd 17: *K2tog, k14; rep from * to end. (90 sts)
Rnd 19: *K2tog, k13; rep from * to end. (84 sts)
Rnd 21: *K2tog, k12; rep from * to end. (78 sts)
Rnd 23: *K2tog, k11; rep from * to end. (72 sts)
Rnd 25: *K2tog, k10; rep from * to end. (66 sts)
Rnd 27: *K2tog, k9; rep from * to end. (60 sts)

Rnd 29: *K2tog, k8; rep from * to end. (54 sts)
Rnd 31: *K2tog, k7; rep from * to end. (48 sts)
Rnd 33: *K2tog, k6; rep from * to end. (42 sts)
Rnd 35: *K2tog, k5; rep from * to end. (36 sts)
Rnd 37: *K2tog, k4; rep from * to end. (30 sts)
Rnd 39: *K2tog, k3; rep from * to end. (24 sts)
Rnd 41: *K2tog, k2; rep from * to end. (18 sts)
Rnd 43: *K2tog, k1; rep from * to end. (12 sts)
Break yarn and draw through remaining 12 sts; tighten to close.

FINISHING

Weave in all ends. A gentle wash and blocking are required to help the decrease lines settle and lay flat.
Fold both corners of the flat Brim section up and sew buttons as shown in the photographs.

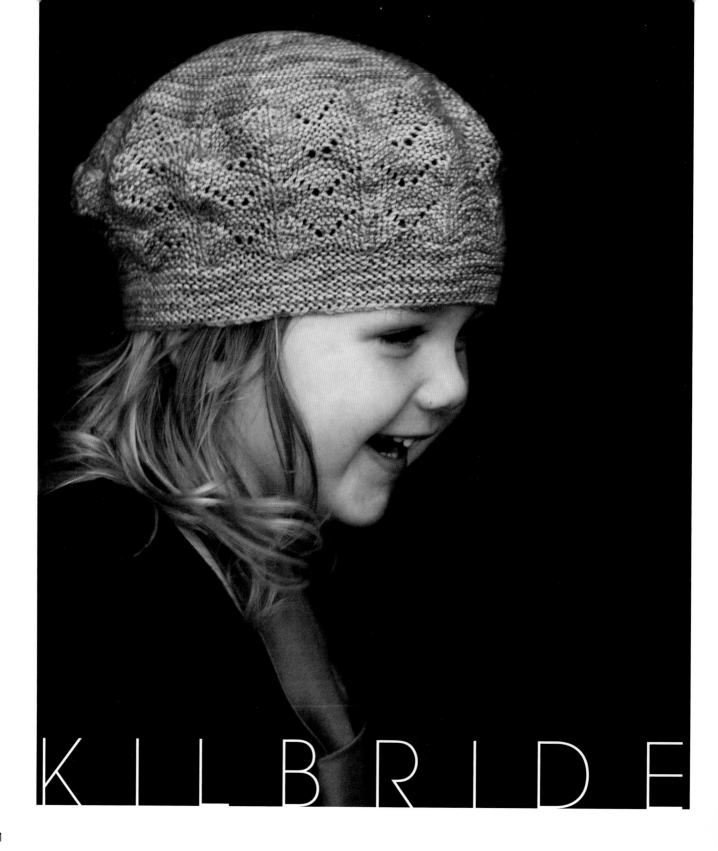

KILBRIDE

SIZES

To fit size: 14 (16, 19, 21, 23) in./35.5 (40.75, 48.25, 53.25, 58.5) cm

Finished size: 11.75 (13.75, 16, 18.25, 20.25) in./29.75 (35, 40.75, 46.25, 51.5) cm

YARN

100 (140, 185, 243, 303) yd./92 (128, 170, 223, 277) m sock/fingering/4-ply weight (super fine) yarn

Additional 49 yd./45 m for a 6 × 6 in./15 × 15 cm swatch in garter st

NEEDLES & NOTIONS

Set of US 1 (2.25 mm) DPNs or circular needle (or size needed to obtain gauge)

US B-1 (2.25 mm) crochet hook

Stitch marker as necessary

Tapestry needle

SAMPLE DETAILS

Shown in Old Maiden Aunt Merino 4ply (400 yd./366 m per 3.5 oz./100 g; 100% superwash merino)

Shown in size 19 in./48.25 cm on model with 18 in./45.75 cm circumference head

GAUGE

31 sts × 42 rows to 4 in./10 cm on US 1 (2.25 mm) needles over St st

30 sts × 58 rows to 4 in./10 cm on US 1 (2.25 mm) needles over garter St

CHART

Page 133

SKILLS REQUIRED

- knit and purl stitches
- knitting in the round
- increases and decreases
- cable cast-on or provisional cast-on (see page 124)
- lace

SPECIAL STITCHES / ABBREVIATIONS

M1P = Pick up the horizontal loop between sts, place it onto the left needle, and then purl into the back of it.

sk2po = Slip next st knitwise, knit following 2 sts together, and then pass slipped st over.

INSTRUCTIONS

Using either cable cast-on method or crochet provisional cast-on method as a permanent cast-on, cast on 88 (104, 120, 136, 152) sts.
Knit all sts, working one row flat, and then join in the round, being careful not to twist sts. Place stitch marker to indicate start of round.

BRIM

Rnd 1: Purl all sts.
Rnd 2: Knit all sts.
Repeat these 2 rounds, creating garter st in the round, until work measures approx. 1 (1.25, 1.25, 1.5, 1.75) in./2.5 (3.25, 3.25, 3.75, 4.5) cm, ending after a Rnd 2, and then work increase round once as follows:
Inc rnd: *P2, M1P; rep from * to end. 132 (156, 180, 204, 228) sts

BODY (Refer to Chart)

Rnd 1: *K1, yo, k4, sk2po, k4, yo; rep from * to end.
Rnd 2 and all even rounds: Purl all sts.
Rnd 3: *K2, yo, k3, sk2po, k3, yo, k1; rep from * to end.
Rnd 5: *K3, yo, k2, sk2po, k2, yo, k2; rep from * to end.
Rnd 7: *K4, yo, k1, sk2po, k1, yo, k3; rep from * to end.
Rnd 9: *K5, yo, sk2po, yo, k4; rep from * to end.
Rnd 10: Purl all sts.
Repeat these 10 rounds until work measures 2.5 (3, 3.5, 4, 4.5) in./6.25 (7.5, 9, 10.25, 11.5) cm, not including the Brim, ending after an even round, and ideally ending after a Rnd 10. You should measure the lace slightly stretched, or gently blocked on the needles.

CROWN PREPARATION

Sizes 14 in./35.5 cm and 21 in./53.25 cm only:

Prep rnd 1: Knit all sts.
Prep rnd 2: *P20 (–, –, 32, –), p2tog; rep from * to end. 126 (–, –, 198, –) sts

CROWN

14 in./35.5 cm size continue with Rnd 23.
16 in./40.75 cm size continue with Rnd 17.
19 in./48.25 cm size continue with Rnd 11.
21 in./53.25 cm size continue with Rnd 7.
23 in./58.5 cm size start at Rnd 1.

Rnd 1 and all odd rounds: Knit all sts.
Rnd 2: *P11, p2tog, p23, p2tog; rep from * to end. (216 sts)
Rnd 4: *P34, p2tog; rep from * to end. (210 sts)
Rnd 6: *P10, p2tog, p21, p2tog; rep from * to end. (198 sts)
Rnd 8: *P31, p2tog; rep from * to end. (192 sts)
Rnd 10: *P9, p2tog, p19, p2tog; rep from * to end. (180 sts)
Rnd 12: *P28, p2tog; rep from * to end. (174 sts)
Rnd 14: *P8, p2tog, p17, p2tog; rep from * to end. (162 sts)
Rnd 16: *P25, p2tog; rep from * to end. (156 sts)
Rnd 18: *P7, p2tog, p15, p2tog; rep from * to end. (144 sts)
Rnd 20: *P22, p2tog; rep from * to end. (138 sts)
Rnd 22: *P6, p2tog, p13, p2tog; rep from * to end. (126 sts)
Rnd 24: *P19, p2tog; rep from * to end. (120 sts)
Rnd 26: *P5, p2tog, p11, p2tog; rep from * to end. (108 sts)
Rnd 28: *P16, p2tog; rep from * to end. (102 sts)
Rnd 30: *P4, p2tog, p9, p2tog; rep from * to end. (90 sts)
Rnd 32: *P13, p2tog; rep from * to end. (84 sts)
Rnd 34: *P3, p2tog, p7, p2tog; rep from * to end. (72 sts)

Rnd 36: *P10, p2tog; rep from * to end. (66 sts)
Rnd 38: *P2, p2tog, p5, p2tog; rep from * to end. (54 sts)
Rnd 40: P7, p2tog; rep from * to end. (48 sts)
Rnd 42: P1, p2tog, p3, p2tog; rep from * to end. (36 sts)
Rnd 44: P4, p2tog; rep from * to end. (30 sts)
Rnd 46: *P2tog, p1, p2tog; rep from * to end. (18 sts)
Rnd 48: *P1, p2tog; rep from * to end. (12 sts)
Break yarn and draw through remaining 12 sts; tighten to close.

FINISHING

Weave in all ends. A gentle wash and blocking are required to help the decrease lines settle and lay flat.

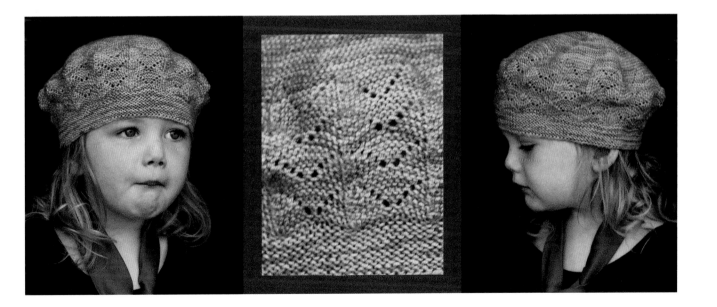

SELKIE

SIZES

To fit sizes: 14 (16, 19, 21, 23) in./35.5 (40.5, 48.25, 53.25, 58.5) cm

Finished size: 12 (14.5, 16.75, 19.25, 21.5) in./30.5 (36.75, 42.5, 49, 54.5) cm

YARN

Yarn A: 29 (41.5, 51.5, 67, 81) yd./27 (38, 47, 61, 74) m worsted weight (medium), plied yarn

Yarn B: 32 (40, 55, 67, 76.5) yd./29 (37, 51, 61, 70) m worsted weight (medium), plied yarn

Additional 22 yd./20 m of Yarn A for a 3 in./7.5 cm pom-pom

Additional 28 yd./26 m for a 6 × 6 in./15 × 15 cm swatch in St st

NEEDLES & NOTIONS

Set of US 6 (4 mm) DPNs or circular needle (or size needed to obtain gauge)

US G-6 (4 mm) crochet hook

Stitch marker as necessary

Tapestry needle

SAMPLE DETAILS

Shown in Lorna's Laces Shepherd Worsted (225 yd./206 m per 4.02 oz./114 g; 100% superwash wool)

Shown in size 21 in./53.25 cm on model with 20.5 in./52 cm circumference head

GAUGE

20 sts × 26 rows to 4 in./10 cm on US 6 (4 mm) needles over St st

20 sts × 40 rows to 4 in./10 cm on US 6 (4 mm) needles over garter st

SKILLS REQUIRED

- knit and purl stitches
- knitting in the round
- increases and decreases
- cable cast-on
- pom-poms
- basic crochet

SPECIAL STITCHES/ABBREVIATIONS

(A) = Work in Yarn A.

(B) = Work in Yarn B.

Sssk = Slip next 3 sts knitwise one by one, and then knit these 3 sts together through the backs of the loops.

INSTRUCTIONS

EAR FLAPS

With Yarn B, cast on 3 sts.
Row 1 (WS): K1, p1, k1.
Row 2 (RS): K1, M1L, k1, M1R, k1. (5 sts)
Row 3: K1, p3, k1.
Row 4: K1, M1L, k3, M1R, k1. (7 sts)
Row 5: K1, p5, k1.
Row 6: K1, M1L, k5, M1R, k1. (9 sts)
Row 7: K1, p7, k1.
Row 8: K1, M1L, k7, M1R, k1. (11 sts)
Row 9: K1, p9, k1.
Row 10: K1, M1L, k9, M1R, k1. (13 sts)
Row 11: K1, p11, k1.
Row 12: K1, M1L, k11, M1R, k1. (15 sts)
Row 13: K1, p13, k1.
Row 14: K1, M1L, k13, M1R, k1. (17 sts)

14 in./35.5 cm size continue with Row 23.
Row 15: K1, p15, k1.
Row 16: K1, M1L, k15, M1R, k1. (19 sts)

16 in./40.5 cm size continue with Row 23.
Row 17: K1, p17, k1.
Row 18: K1, M1L, k17, M1R, k1. (21 sts)

19 in./48.25 cm size continue with Row 23.
Row 19: K1, p19, k1.
Row 20: K1, M1L, k19, M1R, k1. (23 sts)

21 in./53.25 cm size continue with Row 23.
Row 21: K1, p21, k1.
Row 22: K1, M1L, k21, M1R, k1. (25 sts)
Row 23: K1, purl to last st, k1.
Break yarn and hold sts on spare needle ready to join to the Body. Work second ear flap to match.

With spare needles and Yarn A, and knitting across both ear flaps with RS facing, and using cable cast-on method, work the next round as follows, turning work where necessary to keep the cast on continuous with the ear flaps:
Cast on 5 (7, 8, 10, 11) sts, knit 17 (19, 21, 23, 25) sts from first ear flap, cast on 15 (20, 25, 30, 35) sts, knit 17 (19, 21, 23, 25) sts from second ear flap, cast on 6 (7, 9, 10, 12) sts, and then join in the round, taking care not to twist the sts. 60 (72, 84, 96, 108) sts

BRIM

Rnd 1: Purl all sts.
Rnd 2: Knit all sts.
Continuing with Yarn A and starting with Rnd 1, repeat these two rounds until work measures 1.25 (1.5, 1.5, 1.75, 2) in./3.25 (3.75, 3.75, 4.5, 5) cm, ending after a Rnd 1.

BODY

Foundation rnd: (B) *k1, M1L, k10, M1R, k1; rep from * to end. 70 (84, 98, 112, 126) sts

Rnd 1: (B) knit all sts.

Rnd 2: (B) *k1, M1L, k4, ssk, k2tog, k4, M1R, k1; rep from * to end.

Rnd 3: (B) knit all sts.

Rnd 4: (A) *k1, M1L, k4, ssk, k2tog, k4, M1R, k1; rep from * to end.

Rnd 5: (A) purl all sts.

Rnd 6: (B) *k1, M1L, k4, ssk, k2tog, k4, M1R, k1; rep from * to end.

Repeat these six rounds until the body of the hat (excluding the ear flaps) measures approx. 3 (3.5, 3.5, 4, 4.5) in./7.5 (9, 9, 10.25, 11.5) cm, ending after a Rnd 5 (5, 3, 3, 3).

Note: These measurements are to be made when the work is on the needle; the ripple effect of the stitch pattern will cause the length to shorten slightly as it comes off the needles.

CROWN (14 in./35.5 cm and 16 in./40.5 cm sizes)

Rnd 1: (B) *k1, M1L, k3, sssk, k3tog, k3, M1R, k1; rep from * to end. (60, 72 sts)

Rnd 2: (B) knit all sts.

Rnd 3: (B) *k1, M1L, k3, ssk, k2tog, k3, M1R, k1; rep from * to end.

Rnd 4: (B) knit all sts.

Rnd 5: (A) *k1, M1L, k2, sssk, k3tog, k2, M1R, k1; rep from * to end. (50, 60 sts)

Rnd 6: (A) purl all sts.

Rnd 7: (B) *k1, M1L, k2, ssk, k2tog, k2, M1R, k1; rep from * to end.

Rnd 8: (B) knit all sts.

Rnd 9: (B) *k1, M1L, k1, sssk, k3tog, k1, M1R, k1; rep from * to end. (40, 48 sts)

Rnd 10: (B) knit all sts.

Rnd 11: (A) *k1, M1L, k1, ssk, k2tog, k1, M1R, k1; rep from * to end.

Rnd 12: (A) purl all sts.

Rnd 13: (B) *k1, M1L, sssk, k3tog, M1R, k1; rep from * to end. (30, 36 sts)

Rnd 14: (B) knit all sts.

Rnd 15: (B) *k1, M1L, ssk, k2tog, M1R, k1; rep from * to end.

Rnd 16: (B) knit all sts.

Rnd 17: (A) *sssk, k3tog; rep from * to end. (10, 12 sts)

Rnd 18: (A) *p2tog; rep from * to end. (5, 6 sts)

Break yarn and draw through remaining stitches; tighten to close.

CROWN (19 in./48.25 cm, 21 in./53.25 cm, and 23 in./58.5 cm sizes)

Rnd 1: (A) *k1, M1L, k3, sssk, k3tog, k3, M1R, k1; rep from * to end. (84, 96, 108 sts)

Rnd 2: (A) purl all sts.

Rnd 3: (B) *k1, M1L, k3, ssk, k2tog, k3, M1R, k1; rep from * to end.

Rnd 4: (B) knit all sts.

Rnd 5: (B) *k1, M1L, k3, ssk, k2tog, k3, M1R, k1; rep from * to end.

Rnd 6: (B) knit all sts.

Rnd 7: (A) *k1, M1L, k2, sssk, k3tog, k2, M1R, k1; rep from * to end. (70, 80, 90 sts)

Rnd 8: (A) purl all sts.

Rnd 9: (B) *k1, M1L, k2, ssk, k2tog, k2, M1R, k1; rep from * to end.

Rnd 10: (B) knit all sts.

Rnd 11: (B) *k1, M1L, k2, ssk, k2tog, k2, M1R, k1; rep from * to end.

Rnd 12: (B) knit all sts.

Rnd 13: (A) *k1, M1L, k1, sssk, k3tog, k1, M1R, k1; rep from * to end. (56, 64, 72 sts)

Rnd 14: (A) purl all sts.

Rnd 15: (B) *k1, M1L, k1, ssk, k2tog, k1, M1R, k1; rep from * to end.

Rnd 16: (B) knit all sts.

Rnd 17: (B) *k1, M1L, k1, ssk, k2tog, k1, M1R, k1; rep from * to end.

Rnd 18: (B) knit all sts.

Rnd 19: (A) *k1, M1L, sssk, k3tog, M1R, k1; rep from * to end. (42, 48, 54 sts)

Rnd 20: (A) purl all sts.

Rnd 21: (B) *k1, M1L, ssk, k2tog, M1R, k1; rep from * to end.
Rnd 22: (B) knit all sts.
Rnd 23: (B) *k1, M1L, ssk, k2tog, M1R, k1; rep from * to end.
Rnd 24: (B) knit all sts.
Rnd 25: (A) *sssk, k3tog; rep from * to end. (14, 16, 18 sts)
Rnd 26: (A) *p2tog; rep from * to end. (7, 8, 9 sts)
Break yarn and draw through remaining stitches; tighten to close.

POM-POM

Cut two circular pieces measuring 3 in./7.5 cm diameter from thin cardboard. The inner circle should be approximately 1.5 in./3.75 cm. Placing the two pieces of cardboard together, wrap the yarn through the center and around the outer circle, continuing in this manner until the entire piece of cardboard is covered. Continue wrapping the yarn until either the center hole has closed or all the yarn has been used.

Carefully cut the yarn along the edge of the circle to reveal the covered cardboard. Cut all the yarn, and then tie a knot between the two layers of cardboard, effectively tying all the pieces of yarn together, before removing the cardboard. Trim pom-pom before attaching securely to the hat.

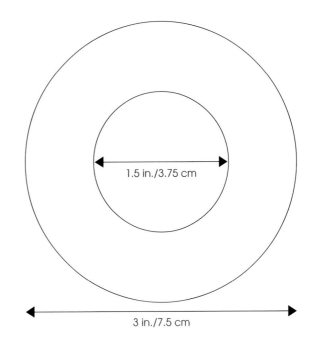

1.5 in./3.75 cm

3 in./7.5 cm

FINISHING

With Yarn B, work one round of single crochet along the lower edge.

Weave in all ends. A gentle wash and blocking are required to help the decrease lines settle and lay flat. It is advisable to block the hat before attaching the pom-pom.

THE RIGHT SIZE

Head sizes vary from person to person but generally fall into the size categories shown below. To be sure, though, one size does not fit all!

To measure your head circumference, wrap a tape measure around the widest part of your head, over your hair, across your forehead and above your ears and around the back, and then around to the front again. Make sure the tape measure is snug. A hat should fit snugly—not too tight or too loose. This is the measurement given for hat sizes, and it is the measurement given for the brim of the hat.

The length (or depth) of a hat will vary between styles, but to know the length of your head in relation to the pattern, measure from your crown to the base of your ear—this will give you your ideal head length for hats.

Patterns contain measurements and sizing based on gauge and number of stitches. If your working gauge is tighter or looser than that given measurement, you may need to adjust your number of stitches accordingly or adjust your needle size.

The finished measurements for hats listed in the patterns may be slightly smaller than those given below, to ensure the fabric is stretched slightly for a snug fit. The actual difference between the finished size of a hat compared to the desired size is usually 2 in./5 cm, or 12 percent. This is the normal amount of negative ease included within Woolly Wormhead knitted and crocheted hat patterns.

The other factor that determines fit is personal choice. Some people like their hats with little or no negative ease for a more casual look, while others prefer a tighter-fitting hat for a sportier look. This preference in fit is also affected by the style of the hat, so do consider how the hat will be worn in relation to the measurements given in the pattern. The patterns include a range of sizes and also the finished measurements—this will help determine which size is the best one to make.

	Premature	Newborn	6 Months	12 Months	Child/Teenager	Adult	Extra Large
Circumference	12 in./ 30.5 cm	14 in./ 35.5 cm	16 in./ 41 cm	18 in./ 46 cm	20 in./ 51 cm	22 in./ 56 cm	24 in./ 61 cm
Length (top of head to base of ear)	4.3 in./ 11 cm	5 in./ 12.5 cm	5.7 in./ 14.5 cm	6.5 in./ 16.5 cm	7.3 in./ 18.5 cm	8.3 in./ 21 cm	9.25 in./ 23.5 cm
Middle ear to middle ear over front/back of head		7.9 in. (20 cm)/ 6.3 in. (16 cm)	8.5 in. (21.5 cm)/ 7.5 in. (19 cm)	9.6 in. (24.5 cm)/ 8.3 in. (21 cm)	11 in. (28 cm)/ 9 in. (23 cm)	12.6 in. (32 cm)/ 9.6 in. (24.5 cm)	13.8 in. (35 cm)/ 10.3 in. (26 cm)

THE RIGHT HAT FOR EVERY HEAD

I'll confess, I'm not a lover of beanie hats. They tend to sit there, squashing your hair, making you look like a bit of an egghead. And I'm a little confused, too, as to why these are the most commonly knitted hat. Don't get me wrong—I'm not anti-beanie; like any hat, beanies have their place. They suit our menfolk well, and they do keep our ears toasty warm when they fit properly, but they are probably the least flattering style for women. Unless you have the right face shape for a close-fitting hat like a beanie, you'll want to consider one of the many other styles available.

I travel to yarn shops with my "Hat Clinic," armed with suitcases full of woolly hats, and I'm often told by knitters that they're not "a hat person"—that hats just don't suit them. Invariably this will be because they haven't found the right style for themselves yet, or they are unsure of how to wear a hat and have given up on seeing the results without trying something different. The aim of my Hat Clinic is to help knitters not only find the right hat but also learn how to wear that hat. And that's my aim here today.

When it comes to wearing a knitted hat—or any hat, for that matter—the one thing we need to consider is balance. For a hat to look good, to suit us, and to keep us warm, it needs to balance with our features. And as wonderfully diverse as we all are, there aren't any hard-and-fast rules about how to achieve this result. Knowing our face shape is a good place to start, as it will give us an idea of our strongest features, and most of us know our face shape already.

HOW MUCH EASE?

For a hat to stay put and do its job, it needs to be smaller than the head. How many beginning hat knitters have labored over their handknits, only to find it won't stay on because it's the same size as their head? It always fills me with sadness when I hear such a tale, and so the subject of fit is an important one.

Ease is the technical word that describes how much bigger or smaller a garment is in relation to the body. In a baggy sweater or loose-fitting cardigan, we want positive ease. When it comes to hats, we're aiming for negative ease. But how much smaller do we really want the hat to be? Ideally, you'd want to aim for somewhere between 2 in./5 cm and 4 in./10 cm of negative ease. How much exactly depends on (a) the fabric or stitch pattern, (b) the fiber content of the yarn, and (c) the look you're aiming for.

Some stitch patterns, such as cables, really don't want to be stretched as much as others, such as ribbing. And some fibers, such as silk or alpaca, don't have as much elastic memory as others, such as wool. As a general rule, if you're knitting a cabled hat from an alpaca/silk blend, you'll be wanting less negative ease. If you're knitting a ribbed hat from pure wool, you'll likely be fine with more negative ease.

Beyond the stitch pattern and yarn used, consider the fit or look. More negative ease creates a skinny or sporty look. Less negative ease creates a more comfortable, casual look. This is as much about personal choice as it is about practicalities, and a good hat knitting pattern will give you the finished size as well as the intended-to-fit size. Armed with this information, you not only know the fit the designer intended for that hat but also are able to decide for yourself which size you'd like to knit.

A word of caution: Too much negative ease can make the hat look too small and cause it to ride up and pop off your head. Too little will make the hat look too big or fall off at the slightest sniff of a breeze . . . which leads us on to our next point . . .

ONE SIZE DOESN'T FIT ALL!

I have another confession: The "one size fits all" tag you often see on hats bothers me—a lot. Because it's just not true.

Yes, knitted fabric stretches. And if you take an average-size hat, then you'll likely get it to fit on much larger heads. But will it really look so lovely when it's stretched to capacity? In fact, will it even look like the same hat? A beret can look more like a beanie on the wrong size head. And how much will it lose in length? Here we have to remember that as we stretch a knitted fabric out widthways, it shortens in length, as the stitches compensate for the pull in the other direction.

Once we've mastered hat sizing, we can start to knit more intricate designs—hats that require a more precise fit and those that use more detailed stitch patterns or are intended for a distinctive or unusual look.

NOT TOO TIGHT!

We all want a hat that stays put and survives the fiercest of winter gales, but that shouldn't mean that the brim of the hat has to pinch our heads oh so tightly. Negative ease will determine fit and how well it stays on, but the choice of knitted brim will make a huge difference in how it looks, without affecting fit.

Ribbed brims are classic; a soft 1 × 1 rib suits women better, whereas a 2 × 2 or wider would be more wisely used on a man's hat. A short-ribbed brim will have the effect of softening the edge, and a deeper brim adds more emphasis to the tight fit and will look more dramatic. One of the most flattering edges I have ever seen doesn't belong in the ribbed category, though, and is often considered insufficient on a hat until it's actually tried: a basic stockinette stitch rolled edge. Sure, ribbing has much more stretch, especially if a ribbed cast-on is used, but do we really want the brim of our hat to be able to stretch through five sizes? It's prudent to remember that a suitably sized hat with a soft brim edge will both fit better and last longer.

THE THING WITH HAIR

Long hair is easy to please with knitted hats, especially long, straight hair. Short hair can be more difficult, as can a lively, curly mane, but that's not to say that these styles don't or won't suit hats. The key with hair is to let it frame your face and work for you. Don't tuck it up and under, or squash it under a tight-fitting hat, causing it to flail out wildly. Even short hair can be of benefit provided it's allowed to be seen. Hair pulled back or tucked away often looks harsh, which in turn will make the hat, and your face, look harsh. Have super-short hair and don't want to look bald with your new knitted hat? Allow a touch of your bangs or a few strands on either side of your head to be visible. This method works every time.

WHERE TO WEAR YOUR HAT

There's been a recent trend to wear hats, particularly berets, toward the back of the head. This can be a flattering look, especially for those with shorter hair or rounder faces, as it can add length to the face. Yet it's not a great look for everyone.

The biggest deal breaker with wearing the hat toward the back is that it isn't necessarily going to keep those ears warm. There's no reason why you can't pull that beret or slouchy hat down onto your forehead, even to eyebrow level, if you want. Provided other points are considered (some hair visible at either the forehead or the ears, or proportion maintained with features, etc.), wearing your hat more snugly provides you with not only a good look but also a warm one.

Wearing your hat lower works particularly well for those with long faces and/or long hair, as it breaks up the length visually, whereas wearing it at back enhances the length, which is something those with long or narrow faces should avoid.

HATS AND GLASSES

Right behind "hats don't suit me," the next most common thing I hear is that glasses and hats don't mix. They do. Glasses are simply another feature to bear in mind, like how you wear your hair or the shape of your face. The main thing to avoid doing with glasses is pulling your hat down so low that the edge of the brim meets the rim of your glasses. You want to allow a little room around your glasses, but not too much. Allow your hair to maintain balance; it's good to see a few wisps between the hat brim and the rim of your glasses.

IT'S ALL A QUESTION OF BALANCE

Really, it is. The trick is to emphasize the good bits and distract from the not-so-good bits. If you have a round face, consider a hat that adds a bit of height without pulling in—tight hats on round faces really are a no-no. Round faces are also better suited to softer-looking brims and should avoid deep or tight ribbing. If you have a long face, consider a hat that adds a bit of width without too much height—such as a beret worn lower over the ears. For a square face, consider something with a more upright structure and, again, avoid anything too tight-fitting beyond the brim. Those with heart-shaped faces are lucky in that they can wear many styles, but they'd still be wise to avoid anything too tight, especially if it's short in length.

Try on a few hats. Be prepared to experiment. Grab hats belonging to your friends/family/neighbors and see what works for you. And don't be afraid to try the hat in different positions. There really is a hat out there for everyone!

ABBREVIATIONS

DPNs = double-pointed needles

k = knit

k1tbl = knit 1 through the back loop

k2tog = knit next 2 sts together

k3tog = knit next 3 sts together

M1 = make 1 (work the same as M1L, below)

M1L = make 1 left-leaning increase (pick up the horizontal bar between sts from front to back with the left needle, and knit into the back of it)

M1R = make 1 right-leaning increase (pick up the horizontal bar between sts from back to front with the left needle, and knit into the front of it)

MM = move marker

p = purl

p2tog = purl next 2 sts together

p3tog = purl next 3 sts together

PM = place marker

rep = repeat

RM = remove marker

rnd = round

RS = right side(s)

sl = slip stitch

ssk = slip, slip, knit (slip next 2 sts knitwise, place back on left-hand needle, and then knit these 2 sts together through the backs of the loops)

ssp = slip, slip, purl (slip next 2 sts knitwise, place back on left-hand needle, put the right-hand needle behind and through the two slipped stitches from left to right and purl them together)

St st = Stockinette stitch

st(s) = stitch(es)

WS = wrong side(s)

yo = yarn over

KITCHENER STITCH GRAFTING IN GARTER STITCH

To ensure that your graft works correctly, you need to set your stitches up correctly. Unlike grafting stockinette stitch, you cannot just bring the edges together; they need to be set up in a particular way. As you look at the needles from the top as shown in step 1, one side should have the ridges right up to the needle and the other should have the ridges sitting away from the needle. If your ridges are the other way around, then you'll want to reverse the instructions (this would be known as "ridge low" grafting). If both needles are the same, you'll want to un-knit one side (this is especially important to remember if you're folding a piece in half to graft—in this case, knit half the row before folding).

When we graft, we work first on the front needle and then on the back needle. It's quite important to remember to stop after step 4 should you need to have a break or tighten up the slack, so that you can start again at a convenient point. Whenever I teach this technique, the most common problem that occurs is stopping midway through the 4-step process, which causes confusion for the knitter.

To start the graft and create the beginning selvedge edge, work steps 2 and 4 once. Then work steps 1–4 until all stitches have been grafted, and finish with steps 1 and 3.

PREPARING FOR THE GRAFT

1. For this graft (known as "ridge high," the front needle (shown here as the bottom needle) has the ridges high and the back needle (shown here as the top needle) has them low. The right sides of work are showing.

2. In most cases when you come to graft garter stitch, the released stitches will be on the back needle, and the yarn will be attached to the front needle.

3. Insert your yarn needle into an inside ridge very close to the first stitch on the back needle.

4. Pull your yarn through. The yarn is now ready to come to the front needle to start the graft.

GRAFTING THE SELVEDGE STITCHES

1. Selvedge stitch 1, front needle: Insert the needle purlwise, pull the yarn through, and then slip the stitch off the needle.

2. Selvedge stitch 1, back needle: Insert the needle purlwise, pull the yarn through, and then slip the stitch off the needle.

GRAFTING GARTER STITCH

3. Stitch 1, front needle: Insert the yarn needle knitwise, pull the yarn through, and then slip the stitch off the needle.

4. Stitch 2, front needle: Insert the needle purlwise, pull the yarn through, but leave the stitch on the needle.

5. Stitch 3, back needle: Insert the needle knitwise, pull the yarn through, and then slip the stitch off the needle.

6. Stitch 4, back needle: Insert the needle purlwise, pull the yarn through, but leave the stitch on the needle.

Repeat steps 3 to 6. You'll notice that what you do on the front needle, you also do on the back needle. To finish the graft, work steps 3 and 5—this creates the final selvedge.

HELPFUL HINTS

Try to take up the slack (i.e., tighten your stitches) every 5 to 10 stitches. Leaving this step until the end will likely cause problems with your tension and cause the graft to look uneven. When taking up the slack, do it slowly, stitch by stitch—don't try pulling from the end, as this will tighten some stitches and not others, and it may even cause your yarn to break!

Always remember to start on the front needle first. If your working yarn is on the front needle, slip it through the base of the first stitch on the back needle to ensure that it connects correctly when starting the graft.

A quick way to remember the garter stitch grafting method is this:
Front needle: knit off, purl on.
Back needle: knit off, purl on.

GERMAN SHORT ROWS IN GARTER STITCH

The German short row method has grown in popularity in recent years, and many knitters prefer this method of short rows over others. As with all approaches to a particular construction technique, not all achieve exactly the same results, so you may choose which will work best or which you prefer.

It's worthwhile to explore a few methods and see which ones give you the best results. Gauge is very much an issue when it comes to short row methods, along with whether you are working flat, whether the short row is on a purl or knit row, or whether the short rows are being worked in the round (in this last case, often a combination of short row methods works best).

TO WORK GERMAN SHORT ROWS

1. Work the number of stitches specified in the pattern, and then you will be performing the short row on the next stitch.

2. Knit the short row stitch. With this method, the stitch I refer to as the "short row stitch" is the same as the stitch that would be wrapped in the w&t (wrap and turn) method.

3. Turn your work so that the short row stitch is the first stitch on the left-hand needle.

4. Slip this stitch to the right-hand needle (this action can also be performed before you turn the work).

5. Take your yarn up and across the back, and pull it very tightly—you will then see two "legs" of the short row stitch on the needle. What you have done here is stretch the stitch underneath the short row stitch right around the needle.

6. Continue pulling the yarn until the legs wrap all the way around the needle and the yarn is in the correct place to work a knit stitch.

7. It's important to maintain the tightness of this maneuver before knitting back across the stitches to the end of the row.

8. Once all the short rows have been worked, they will look like this—each short row stitch has two legs.

WORKING ACROSS THE SHORT ROW

Once you've created your short rows, you'll need to work across them all to close them and give your work a neat finish. Compared to working the wrap and turn method, this part is much quicker and easier than picking up the wrap.

9. Knit as instructed until you reach your first short row stitch.

10. Insert your needle under both legs of the short row stitch as shown—you will knit these together. Continue to do this with all the short row stitches.

11. This is how all of the short rows look from the front.

12. And this is how all the short rows look from the back.

Compared to the wrap and turn method, the front of the work is very neat with tightly worked stitches, and there's a more visible ridge across the back. If you are working your short rows consecutively, such as the crown on a sideways knit hat, then your short rows will consistently be on the same side of your work. However, if you also have short rows at the brim of a sideways knit hat, or are working short rows at either end of a piece of flat knitting, then the back side of this method will appear on the right side of your work. For one or two stitches, this will likely not be noticeable, especially in garter stitch, but it's important to be aware of this difference.

With the wrap and turn method you have more flexibility, as you would pick up the wrap from whichever side is the right side and your short rows would then be consistent in appearance from the front of your work.

PROVISIONAL CAST-ON

If you are knitting a sideways constructed hat and wish for a professional seam-free finish, then this is the cast-on for you. Working hand in hand with Kitchener stitch, this cast-on method allows you to cast on "live" stitches that are later removed and grafted. The chain crochet provisional cast-on is fairly well known, but the method of working it directly onto the needle isn't—trying to find the right bump along a crocheted chain to pick up as a stitch can be difficult, and if the wrong bump is picked up, the provisional cast-on isn't as easily removed. Crocheting the stitches directly onto the needle, as shown here, saves a lot of time and effort! Once you have finished the body of your knitting, this cast-on is easily removed, although it is advisable to remove the chain stitch by stitch, so as to avoid dropping any stitches.

To do this provisional cast-on, you will need a crochet hook and some waste yarn. The amount of waste yarn needed will vary depending on your project, but for most of Woolly Wormhead's sideways hats, 2 yards/2 meters is plenty. When choosing your waste yarn, use something that isn't fuzzy—something without grip. A wool yarn may well start to felt with handling, and it can be difficult to remove. Cotton or other smooth yarns are best for this job. The crochet hook should be the same size as the needles you will use, although one a little larger will help make the chain easier to remove at the end. The same goes for the waste yarn—use one the same gauge as (or slightly heavier than) the yarn you will be using in your knitting.

1. Using your waste yarn, make a slipknot and slip it onto your crochet hook. Hold the hook in front of the needle, taking the working yarn behind the needle. With the hook, catch the working yarn at the front.

2. Pull the working yarn through the loop on the hook—this will form your first stitch. Move the working yarn between the needle and hook so that it is behind the needle again, and repeat these two steps until you have the required number of stitches.

3. Once you have the right number of stitches, pull the remaining loop on the crochet hook until it becomes very large, tie a knot in it, and then break your yarn.

Your provisional cast-on is now complete, and you are ready to knit! This is how the cast-on looks after a few rows of knitting.

When you have finished the body of knitting and wish to remove the provisional cast-on, carefully undo the knot in the waste yarn and start to remove the chain. Don't rip the chain out quickly—you could lose or drop stitches—so it is best to remove these carefully, one by one. If the stitches around the provisional cast-on are complex and it's difficult to see where to insert your needle to grab the stitch, gently stretch the chain and the knitting in different directions so that the loop of the stitch you need to pick up will be more visible.

If there is any time when you need to bind off and then cast on again in a piece of knitting, this cast-on method works perfectly, as it mirrors a regular bind-off very nicely. Instead of using waste yarn, you will use your working yarn. The slipknot you would normally create to start the provisional cast-on will be replaced as the last stitch knitted before the cast-on commences; slip this knitted stitch onto the crochet hook, and work as above. When you have cast on enough stitches less one, slip the stitch on the hook back onto the needle, and your cast-on section is now ready. This method works particularly well when you need to cast on mid-row.

TWO-COLOR KITCHENER STITCH GRAFTING IN GARTER STITCH

The key to a successful graft is in the preparation and in ensuring that you have the correct number of stitches in each yarn or color segment before starting the graft.

1. As you remove the provisional cast-on, you will notice that you are one stitch short on the released stitches. The usual advice would be to make up that extra stitch at the edge of the work, such as at the crown edge of a sideways knit hat, but when we are grafting across two colors, we need to ensure that the missing stitch is replaced in the right section. In this example, the lighter-colored yarn is one stitch short.

2. If you look at the stitches after they have been released, you will notice an extra loop next to where the yarn changed color—this should be in the yarn that has the missing stitch. Insert your needle into the loop from front to back in order to ensure the new stitch has the same orientation as the others. At this point you will also have the yarn tail of the second colored yarn—where

this sits depends on whether you joined the new yarn on a right side or wrong side row, but you'll want to slip it through the loop so that it sits at the front of the work as shown.

3. Then take the yarn toward the back, to the right of the loop—this is done to make your new stitch look the same as all the other stitches from the right side of the work.

4. Once all of the stitches are on the needle together, you are ready to graft. In this example, the stitches that have been released will be on the back needle, and the graft will start with the lighter-colored yarn.

5. Work a regular garter stitch graft across the stitches until you reach the point of having only one stitch remaining in the first yarn. Insert your needle knitwise and slip the stitch off the needle—this is the first stitch of the graft, which is shown as step 3 in the garter grafting tutorial on page 120.

6. Then, using the same yarn and a tapestry needle, insert your needle knitwise into the stitch on the back needle and slip it off—this is step 5 of the garter graft, the third stitch. What you are essentially doing is working to close the graft of the first yarn, as you would when you come to the end of a graft on a flat piece of knitting.

7. Now change to the second yarn, and treat this as you would when you are starting the graft at the beginning, by working the second stitch (step 4) of the graft. Insert your needle purlwise into the next stitch, and then pull the yarn through, leaving the stitch on the needle.

8. Insert the needle purlwise into the first stitch on the back needle and pull the yarn through, leaving the stitch on the needle—this is step 6 of the graft, the fourth stitch. You will now return to step 3 of the graft on the first stitch on the front needle, and continue grafting across the remaining stitches with the regular garter stitch graft.

This method of changing yarns is quite simple in practice—you simply perform the finishing steps on the final stitches of the first yarn, and then restart the graft with the new yarn. This principle can be applied to stockinette stitch and other stitches. As long as the preparation is done—making up for the missing stitch at the correct point—the graft will not jog across the yarn changes. In addition to using this method for a change in yarn color, it can be used for a change in yarn thickness or texture. You can perform this graft across as many color changes as necessary, allowing you to create a perfectly invisible seam across Fair Isle or stranded work (there will always only be one color section that has one stitch short, so you will only need to perform the preparation once).

NOTE

You can find even more knitting technique tutorials on Woolly Wormhead's website: www.woollywormhead.com.

INTERCONNECTED
Page 14

KEY

| I | = Knit on RS.

| − | = Knit on WS.

| ∞ | = Work short row. For the wrap and turn method, this is the stitch that is wrapped. For the German short row method, this is the double-leg stitch.

| S | = Slip stitch purlwise with yarn in front.

CHART 1

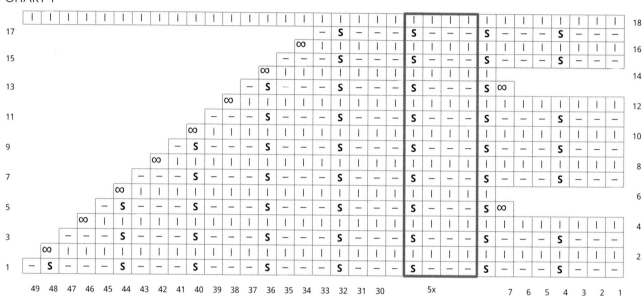

CHART 2

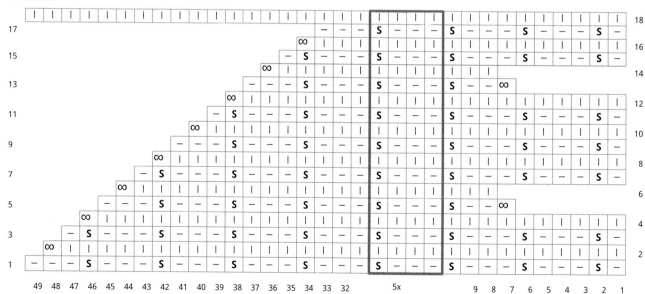

Page 22

CHART

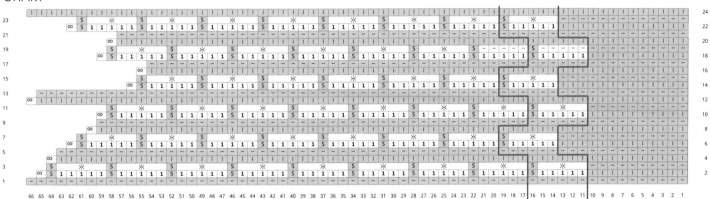

KEY

☐ = With Yarn A, knit on RS.

☐ = With Yarn A, knit on WS.

☐ = With Yarn B, knit on WS.

☐ = With Yarn B, knit on RS.

☐ = K1, yo.

☐ = Slip stitch with yarn at back on RS and yarn in front on WS (a stitch in Yarn A will be carried).

☐ ※ ☐ = Slip 5 sts to right-hand needle, dropping extra loops; slip these 5 sts back to left-hand needle and then (k1, yo, k1, yo, k1) into all 5 sts together through the backs of the loops.

∞ = Work short row. For the wrap and turn method, this is the stitch that is wrapped. For the German short row method, this is the double-leg stitch.

FLORALYS

Page 50

CHART

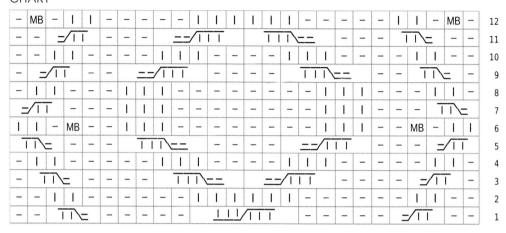

KEY

☐ = Knit.

☐ = Purl.

☐ = T3B. Slip next st onto cable needle and hold at back of work, knit next 2 sts, and then purl stitch from cable needle (right twist).

☐ = T3F. Slip next 2 sts onto cable needle and hold at front of work, purl next st, and then knit 2 sts from cable needle (left twist).

☐ = T5B. Slip next 2 sts onto cable needle and hold at back of work, knit next 3 sts, and then purl 2 sts from cable needle (right twist).

☐ = T5F. Slip next 3 sts onto cable needle and hold at front of work, purl next 2 sts, and then knit the 3 sts from cable needle (left twist).

☐ = C6B. Slip next 3 sts onto cable needle and hold at back of work, knit next 3 sts on left-hand needle, and then knit 3 sts from the cable needle (right cross).

MB = MB. Knit into the front and then back, then front and back, and then into the front of the next stitch. Turn work. Slip 1, p4, turn work. K2tog, k3tog, pass st from k2tog over and off the needle.

130

TANGLED RIVER
Page 54

CHART 1

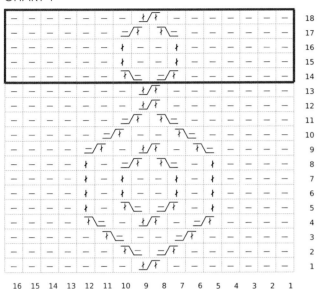

KEY

$\boxed{|}$ = Knit.

$\boxed{-}$ = Purl.

$\boxed{\not|}$ = Knit stitch through back loop.

$\boxed{\wedge}$ = Knit next 2 sts together.

$\boxed{\triangle}$ = Purl next 2 sts together.

$\boxed{\triangle}$ = Slip next 2 sts knitwise, and then purl these 2 sts together through the backs of the loops.

$\boxed{\wedge}$ = Slip next 2 sts knitwise, and then knit these 2 sts together through the backs of the loops.

$\boxed{\not|/\not|}$ = C2B. Slip next st onto cable needle and hold at back of work, knit next st through the back loop, and then knit the st from the cable needle through the back loop (right cross).

$\boxed{-/\not|}$ = T2B. Slip next st onto cable needle and hold at back of work, knit next st through the back loop, and then purl the st from the cable needle (right twist).

$\boxed{\not|\backslash-}$ = T2F. Slip next st onto cable needle and hold at front of work, purl next st, and then knit next st through the back loop (left twist).

CHART 2

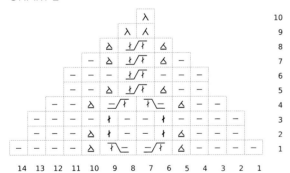

ERICA

Page 58

CHART 1

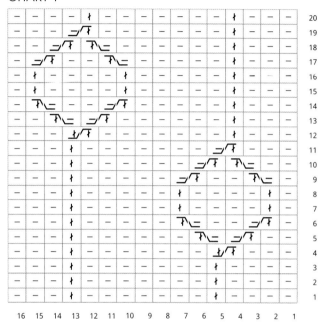

CHART 2

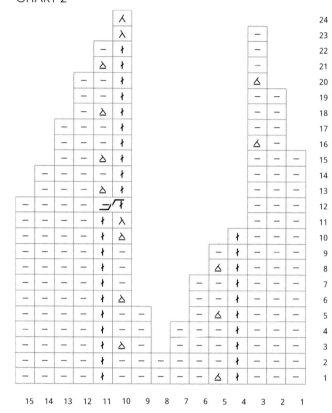

KEY

☐ = Purl.

Ϯ = Knit stitch through back loop.

⋏ = Knit next 2 sts together.

⋏ = Purl next 2 sts together.

△ = Slip next 2 sts knitwise, and then purl these 2 sts together through the backs of the loops.

λ = Slip next 2 sts knitwise, and then knit these 2 sts together through the backs of the loops.

C2B. Slip next st onto cable needle and hold at back of work, knit next st through the back loop, and then knit the st from the cable needle through the back loop (right cross).

T2B. Slip next st onto cable needle and hold at back of work, knit next st through the back loop, and then purl the st from the cable needle (right twist).

T2F. Slip next st onto cable needle and hold at front of work, purl next st, and then knit next st through the back loop (left twist).

INCATENATO

Page 90

CHART

12	11	10	9	8	7	6	5	4	3	2	1	
I	I	I	I	I	I	I	I	I	I	I	I	27
—	—	—	—	—	—	—	—	—	—	—	—	26
I	I	I	I	I	I	I	I	I	I	I	I	25
S	—	—	—	—	—	—	—	—	—	S	S	24
S	I	I	I	I	I	I	I	I	I	S	S	23
—	S	—	—	—	—	—	—	—	S	—	—	22
I	S	I	I	I	I	I	I	I	S	I	I	21
S	—	S	—	—	—	—	S	—	S	S		20
S	I	S	I	I	I	I	S	I	S	S		19
—	S	—	S	—	—	—	S	—	S	—	—	18
I	S	I	S	I	I	I	S	I	S	I	I	17
—	—	—	—	—	S	—	—	—	—	—	—	16
I	I	I	I	I	S	I	I	I	I	I	I	15
—	—	—	—	S	—	S	—	—	—	—	—	14
I	I	I	I	S	I	S	I	I	I	I	I	13
—	—	—	—	—	S	—	—	—	—	—	—	12
I	I	I	I	I	S	I	I	I	I	I	I	11
—	S	—	S	—	—	—	S	—	S	—	—	10
I	S	I	S	I	I	I	S	I	S	I	I	9
S	—	S	—	—	—	—	S	—	S	S		8
S	I	S	I	I	I	I	I	S	I	S	S	7
—	S	—	—	—	—	—	—	—	S	—	—	6
I	S	I	I	I	I	I	I	I	S	I	I	5
S	—	—	—	—	—	—	—	—	—	S	S	4
S	I	I	I	I	I	I	I	I	I	S	S	3
—	—	—	—	—	—	—	—	—	—	—	—	2
I	I	I	I	I	I	I	I	I	I	I	I	1

KEY

☐ I = With Yarn A, knit.

☐ — = With Yarn A, purl.

☐ I = With Yarn B, knit.

☐ — = With Yarn B, purl.

☐ S = Slip stitch with yarn at back (a stitch in Yarn A will be carried).

☐ S = Slip stitch with yarn at back (a stitch in Yarn B will be carried).

KILBRIDE

Page 104

CHART

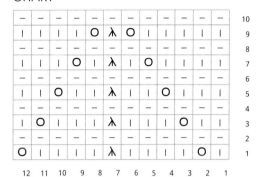

12	11	10	9	8	7	6	5	4	3	2	1	
—	—	—	—	—	—	—	—	—	—	—	—	10
I	I	I	I	O	λ	O	I	I	I	I	I	9
—	—	—	—	—	—	—	—	—	—	—	—	8
I	I	I	O	I	λ	I	O	I	I	I	I	7
—	—	—	—	—	—	—	—	—	—	—	—	6
I	I	O	I	I	λ	I	I	O	I	I	I	5
—	—	—	—	—	—	—	—	—	—	—	—	4
I	O	I	I	I	λ	I	I	I	O	I	I	3
—	—	—	—	—	—	—	—	—	—	—	—	2
O	I	I	I	I	λ	I	I	I	I	O	I	1

KEY

☐ I = Knit.

☐ — = Purl.

☐ O = Yarn over.

☐ λ = Slip next st knitwise, then knit following 2 sts together, and then pass slipped st over.

YARN SOURCES

A big thank you for the yarn support for this book goes to the following companies:

Fyberspates
https://fyberspates.com/home

Ripples Crafts
https://www.ripplescrafts.com/

Whimzy Yarn
https://www.whimzy.co.uk/

Lorna's Laces
https://www.lornaslaces.net/

Nua Yarn
http://nuayarn.com/

Old Maiden Aunt
https://oldmaidenaunt.com/

Meadow Yarn
https://www.meadowyarn.co.uk/

Jamieson & Smith
http://www.shetlandwoolbrokers.co.uk/

Neighborhood Fiber Co.
https://neighborhoodfiberco.com/#

Babylonglegs
https://babylonglegs.co.uk

ABOUT THE AUTHOR

With an instinctive flair for unusual construction and a passion for innovation, **Woolly Wormhead** is a designer whose patterns are trusted and celebrated by knitters all over the world. As a designer, Woolly is driven by a need to create and develop her understanding of three-dimensional form. Communicating her ideas and sharing her specialized knowledge with her followers are key to Woolly's success as a designer.

woollywormhead.com

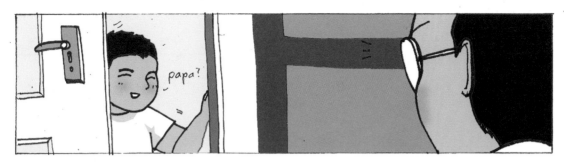

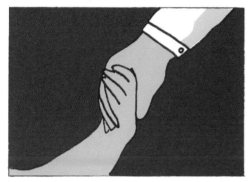

for the natural environment, for the young ones...

... and generations to come.

END.